MBA at 58

And Other
IMPROBABLE
STORIES

Volume One

DOUG KEIPPER

MBA at 58, MBAat58, MBAat58.com and www.MBAat58.com
Copyright © 2020 by Doug Keipper

ISBN (Print): 978-1-09834-480-1
ISBN (eBook): 978-1-09834-481-8

Printed in USA by
BookBaby Publishing.
www.bookbaby.com

Dedication

This book is dedicated to all the book's warriors that made sacrifices and overcame rejection, setbacks, obstacles, disappointment, depression, tears, sleepless nights, anxiety, horrible bosses, and bizarre family members. Without your stories, we couldn't encourage each other. When I told you that I was writing a book and wanted your story – you believed me. You believed that I was going to pull it off. You willingly jumped on Team Doug, and said "let's go!" Thank you.

Thank you to my transcriptionist at Upwork, Samantha Simoneau; my daughter, part-time editor and almost a doctor, Rebecca Keipper; my lovely wife of thirty-one years Nan (chapter on her coming in volume 2); and my daughter Rachel, who travels the world, and inspires us all.

I have to throw a shout out to Emma. She was a boss I had that was three and then four levels up from me. She always gave me a smile and words of encouragement during my schooling. When I told her I was taking statistics, she sent out an email to three people in the department who had master's degrees in statistics, and TOLD them to answer my questions. When I was taking my management class, I asked for thirty minutes of her time over lunch. She graciously welcomed me up to the big tower, and we dined on homemade sandwiches and discussed strategies when taking on a new role. When I had a friend of my daughter in the office who was a third-year accounting major with a 3.8 GPA, she took thirty minutes to talk about possible career choices and career paths. We sat in her office and discussed our aging mothers, their eventual deaths, and being caretakers. She moved on from the bank, but still keeps in touch during college football season, and even responds to my emails when surveying friends and family about the *MBA at 58* logos. Emma, thank you for all of your encouragement. A big part of this degree, and even this book, is a testimony to your leadership in developing people.

As F. Scott Fitzgerald says "For what it's worth: it's never too late to be whoever you want to be. I hope you live a life you're proud of, and if you find that you're not, I hope you have the strength to start over"

Table of Contents

Foreword

I first met Doug in a conversation something like this:

Doug: "I review bank records to catch tax cheats, drug dealers, hookers, pimps and terrorists."

Me: "Oh, that's interesting. Here's my kid, I'll be back in an hour."

It's not quite as alarming as it may sound. Doug volunteers at the local church we both attend, and it was there that I first remember meeting Doug as I dropped off my one-year-old daughter and rushed into church. In some ways, he's the most unlikely nursery volunteer at church you will ever meet. In other ways, that's what makes him the best nursery volunteer at church. He's eccentric, conversational, and willing to do just about anything to get a laugh (and/or keep kids from crying uncontrollably – both of which are realistic goals for church nursery). Much of our interactions consist of these types of conversation snippets, where we slowly learned more about each other. I learned about his daughters, particularly his pride in their school success and the "love of his life" (as he describes his wife) and, most importantly, I SAW one of the most genuine people I've ever met. How many fifty-something men do you see changing diapers and calming crying babies in the church nursery?

In these conversations, Doug learned about the "other life" I lead beyond that of the somewhat stereotypical suburban female with a husband, two daughters, and a dog, driving an SUV. That is, "by day" I'm Dr. O'Neal, a faculty member at a research-intensive university, regularly publishing complex statistical analyses in well-respected, peer-reviewed journals, while directing research grants with annual budgets nearing a million dollars. I found Doug's interest in my work refreshing, as most who know me outside of my work seem unsure of what to make of it or how to integrate it in their understanding of, and interactions with, me. In one of our conversations, Doug asked what I study, I told him about my primary research areas, including risk and resilience among families facing acute or chronic adversity. And that is when I began to hear his passion for writing this book and his "popcorn theory". Now, as a family scientist, a good theory is fascinating, and his piqued my interest. My training teaches me to question any theory's veracity, and test and authenticate it, even at a basic level. For instance, I began to weigh the theory proposition with my own experiences and previous research I have read or conducted... "He's on to something," I remember thinking.

And so, my thesis for this foreword is a simple statement – it's an endorsement for the ideas and theory of my friend, Doug, from both of the "hats" I wear – that of Dr. O'Neal, the academic, and Catie, the everyday mom/wife. Doug is a genuine and real person in a relatively superficial world, with a knack for seeing people for who they really are, and all sides of them. The ideas and narratives he shares in this book are examples of him "seeing" people, noticing they have a story to tell, motivating them to tell it, and curating the telling of their stories in a manner that facilitates their own growth, and hopefully the growth of others. What academics have termed a "growth mindset" (Dweck, 2015) and "grit" (Duckworth, 2016),

Doug has made into his life outlook. May we all have a passion for lifelong learning.

An academic's preface to this book.

It's the intersection of risk and resilience where the real transformations happen...what Andy Stanley may call "the messy middle." You see, resilience is defined as experiencing crisis or stress and overcoming it, to either a) return to baseline (pre-crisis) functioning, or b) exceed baseline functioning.

That second part (b) has also been referred to as post-traumatic growth – the idea that exposure to trauma (or for the sake of argument, crisis/hardship more generally) can not only be overcome but can prompt something better than what previously was.

As a society, we are quick to adopt these sorts of ideas when it comes to physical injury/improvement, but less so when it comes to less obvious stress. Examples of physical pain mottos: No pain, no gain; no guts, no glory.

My Biographical Statement

Dr. Catherine Walker O'Neal, Ph.D. is an Associate Research Scientist in the Department of Human Development and Family Science at the University of Georgia. Her research focuses on the interplay of risk and resilience among families facing acute or chronic stressors over the life course to inform evidence-based outreach efforts. Overall, her work utilizes advanced statistical methods to identify protective factors that support families, such as formal programming and informal networks of support, and examines change over time for families' and individuals' relational, physical, and mental health. Dr. O'Neal has extensive training in the use of quantitative methods to evaluate contextual and ecological effects, including program effects, on individual and family well-being. In 2016, she co-authored a book entitled *Higher-Order Growth Curves and Mixture Modeling with Mplus: A Practical Guide*, which speaks to her ability to understand how and why change occurs over time and convey that information to multiple audiences. One specific area of her research is how stress in early life stages impacts subsequent health and well-being at later life stages. For instance, her research demonstrated that adverse child experiences in the family of origin are linked to adults' life context (including their mental health, physical health, social connections, and parenting quality), which, in turn, has implications for their adolescents' mental, physical, and relational health (O'Neal et al., 2016, published in *American Journal of Orthopsychiatry*). In this manner, her work addresses the persistence of early life experiences and their transmission to others. Dr. O'Neal has published over eighty-six peer-reviewed manuscripts, in addition to co-authoring books, book chapters, and policy briefs, and regularly presenting at national conference presentations. She regularly publishes her research in well-respected family science journals, such as *Journal of Marriage and Family, Family Psychology, Family Process*, and *American Journal of Community Psychology*.

Preface

To get something you never had, you have to do something you never did.

When I was ten years old, I took over my brother's lawn cutting business. It was lonely, boring and hot cutting grass all summer. I was not a fan. In 1975, Indiana required you to be fourteen years old to pump gas at a marina. At thirteen, I got my first real paycheck working weekends at a marina in the fall, scrubbing algae off the bottom of boats with muriatic acid, before they winterized the engine for winter storage. Oh, sure, let the thirteen-year-old kid breathe muriatic acid for sixteen hours on the weekend, but don't let him touch a gas pump. The following summer I pumped gas and cleaned boats, forty hours a week. There were three of us my age at Cooper's Marina on beautiful Lake Tippecanoe in northern Indiana. Mercury Marine had a distribution center and service school near my home in Ft. Wayne. I was the only one of the three kids who went to service school to learn how to work on the motors. There were three spring breaks during high school and college that I went to service school to learn how to fix Mercury and Evinrude outboard engines. I still use some of those troubleshooting skills to this day. I've always had the curiosity of a cat – how does a motor work – how does a bank work – how does the stock market work – how do you publish a book!! I've had a good work ethic, but without the right grade point average or proper direction, you can get lost pretty easily. This book is eleven stories about getting back on track. At any age.

Introduction

Your life unfolds in proportion to your courage.

—Danielle LaPorte

The purpose of this book is to find your mentor, and to give you hope and encouragement to make it through whatever stumbling blocks you have. Somebody has been in your shoes. Somebody has overcome the obstacles you are facing right now. I want you to get inspired that you can change your mindset, change your direction, and change your life. In this book, you will hear my story, as well as the stories of my friends, business associates and neighbors. I hope you can identify with one, or more, of them.

When I announced in August 2016, at age fifty-four, that I signed up to begin my MBA, I was fortunate to be showered with a hundred percent positive encouragement. Several people my age said they couldn't do it. They couldn't go back to school. They were impressed that I was stepping up to the long road ahead. In June of 2020 I finished my degree, and I'm excited to share my story with you.

What's your dream? Chapter 2? Version 2.0, 3.0, or maybe it's 5.5? What is your timeline? Is it a someday goal or is it a "we got to get this done" goal?

Let's make today day one.

Let's get you to believe in you.

What you are ultimately going to read is a book about people changing their mindset. According to world-renowned Stanford University psychologist Carol S. Dweck, Ph.D. in her book *Mindset: The New Psychology of Success*, 2015: You can either have a fixed mindset (I'm always going to be _____) or you can have a growth mindset (in my case – I'm going back to school). I want you to see how each voice in this book changed their mindset, and they changed their outcome. They had a new vision of their future. You can use Dweck's research to help shape the future of yourself, your spouse, children, coworkers, parents, or next-door neighbor.

"If you manage people or are a parent (which is a form of managing people), drop everything and read *Mindset*."

—Guy Kawasaki, author of *The Art of the Start 2.0*

MBA at 58 may give you the individual stories that apply to a specific set of circumstances, and encourage change. If you would like to share your story for a future volume of this book series, please contact me at www.MBAat58.com.

Chapter 1

My Story

"I graduated high school in the one-third of my class that made the top two-thirds possible."

—Doug Keipper

My parents were high school sweethearts from a Chicago suburb called Lockport. Dad decided to go to the University of Illinois, and mom decided to go too, so they could be together. Their studies were short lived. Dad soon joined the Army to serve in World War II, and mom left college after a year because her friends were making a hundred dollars a month in the typing pool, and she could make three hundred dollars a month as a model. College cost a thousand dollars per year, and she didn't see the point in spending a thousand dollars per year for college when she could make better money as a model. Her parents never forgave her for spending a thousand dollars of their money on that first year of college. World War II ended about eighteen months after dad enlisted. He was honorably discharged with the Medal of Freedom, and given the G.I. Bill to attend college. They found a small technical college in northern Indiana, now called Indiana Tech, where dad could get a mechanical engineering degree.

They were thirty-five when I was born, the youngest of four children. We all lived in Huntington, Indiana, a beautiful small town in northeast Indiana. I walked ten blocks to school. The dentist was an eight-block walk the other way. I can still point to the area of the parking lot at Huntington North High School where I learned to ride a two-wheel bike. My buddies and I rode Schwinn Sting Ray bicycles like we were in a gang. I could walk or ride my bike to the Stop 'N Go convenience store and to all of my friends' houses. We could go sledding on the hill at St. Mary's Catholic Church. It was a seemingly idyllic small-town life.

When I was in the sixth grade, we moved from Huntington, Indiana (population 15,000) to Fort Wayne (population 170,000). In Huntington, there was one high school, but Ft. Wayne had several high schools of various sizes. I was in a new town, a new school, and I knew no one. This new town was over ten times bigger, and I didn't know every street like I used to. I felt a little overwhelmed. Luckily, we moved into a large subdivision of townhomes. There were lots of kids to meet of various ages, all within walking distance. The downside was, there were lots of kids to distract you from homework, and you could easily waste hours of time. We were fortunate to have tennis courts, a basketball court, and pools for the summertime. During the winter there was a pond for ice skating, and small hill for sledding. It was a good way to meet new people, and I still keep in touch with a few of them to this day.

I had good attendance at school because I learned best by listening. When the teacher assigned twenty pages of algebra, that just wasn't going to happen. First of all, the voice in my head reading it sounded like Charlie Brown's teacher: "Mamawwaa mamawwaa mamawwaa." Second, it was boring. Third, it was a sunny day outside, and plenty of people around to waste some time. Maybe I had an attention disorder back before they called it that. I listened in class and I did most of the homework. By the time I was a senior in high school, I was a cheerleader (indoor practice with the prettiest girls in school – great decision!) and served in Student Council as president of the senior class. Academically, I was in the one-third of my high school class that made the top two-thirds possible. The SAT comprised two sections at the time, Math and Verbal, each scoring between 200-800, with 1600 being a perfect score. I scored an impressive 500 in the math section (average) and 350 in the verbal section (definitely below average) for a combined 850 score. According to my mother, my other siblings were within 50 points of each other, and I was "a little lower than them".

Ball State University in Muncie, Indiana was gracious for accepting me in late September of my senior year of high school. In college, against all odds, I graduated on time in four years. There was a little detour during college that I can't skip over. During my junior year, I was at a fraternity party and decided I needed to get on my roommate's shoulders on the dance floor. One thing led to another, and I fell off backwards and landed on my head on a concrete floor. I broke my neck, and was paralyzed from the neck down. Long story short, I had surgery, and with lots of love and physical therapy, regained all of my mobility. I missed spring semester, but made it all up with summer school. I graduated with a stellar 2.7 GPA in marketing, but I did it on time. In college, I worked hard and applied myself, but not to my studies. I never missed a party, and was truly a stereotypical fraternity brother. Studying was low on my priority list, and my GPA severely limited my choices for a good job after college. My feeble attempts at making up for my GPA with involvement in student government and other organizations, as well as my obviously winning personality, were somehow not enough to impress future employers.

From middle school to the time I graduated college, my dad's success in rising up in the ranks of corporate life had earned him a lot of work-related stress. Additionally, my older siblings set the bar high for me. My oldest brother went off to college when I was five, my sister did the same when I was eight, and my second oldest brother studied hard and succeeded in architecture school. My father, now under the constant pressure of corporate life, drank too much and was harsh with me, even becoming verbally abusive. In his defense, I probably deserved some tough love. I thought, because everybody ahead of me was succeeding, life would be easy and it would just come naturally. As described above, success did not come easily or naturally because I didn't put in the work. I needed some healthy constructive criticism, but his words went too far. When I was twenty-two and just out of college, dad sought help, got sober, and stayed sober until his death eighteen years later. It was like I had two different dads. As much as I enjoyed my new dad, the verbal abuse of my youth felt written in stone. Several books and classes about the emotional scars of Adult Children of Alcoholics made a big impact on my life. My siblings were out of the house by that stage in his life. They don't remember the verbal abuse like I do, but my mom was certainly aware of it. She and I talked of it when I became her legal guardian and power of attorney in the last years of her life.

My graduation present from college was a one-way U-Haul. "Son Douglas, anywhere you want to go – One Way." I repeated that mantra to both of my daughters starting in middle school. My U-Haul and I headed south to Atlanta because I had experienced all the snow I needed for the rest of my life. 1984 faced a recession, and I was ten hours from home in Georgia with a 2.7 GPA. This winning combination left me with, as I like to say, "suck jobs" for ten years: entry-level sales jobs with high turnover.

As a side note, I should have gone to work for Home Depot. It was brand new and I loved walking the isles even though I lived in an apartment and had no use for ninety-nine percent of their inventory. I liked the idea of working there, but I had a college degree, so I thought I had to have a suit-and-tie job. I didn't want to disappoint my parents. People tell me that with a marketing degree, I would have been transferred into the home office within a year of working in the store. Truth be known, if I had gone to Home Depot at store number three and been in the home office at age twenty-four, or twenty-five, I'd be retired by now, and you wouldn't have this book because I either would have gotten the MBA a long time ago or I wouldn't have needed it. Moral of the story – never turn down investigating a company that piques your interest.

I had a career around mortgage banking, retail banking, and selling software to banks. Our two daughters were raised in metropolitan Atlanta. When they left for college at the University of Georgia (Go Dawgs), my wife and I could both work from home, so we fled the oppressive traffic of the suburbs and moved eighty-three miles east to Lake Oconee. A month after we moved there, I got laid off. Once again, I was in a new town and knew no one. This time, instead of being in a large city with plentiful opportunity, I was in a small town and knew nobody. On the surface, I was happy to be at the lake, but deep down, I was full of despair and loneliness.

I spent eight hours each day searching for and applying for various banking and software sales jobs. I drove to towns up to an hour away, walked into every bank, and filled out an application. At night I played tennis at the local country club that allowed outside guests. I tried to keep my unemployment a secret because I didn't want to be the unknown new guy begging for a job. In hindsight, I should have networked better than I did. My wife and I joined a church and Bible study group, something that had been important to us throughout our marriage and family life. My adult Bible study group was accepting of my stage in life, and prayed for me several times. They gave me a lot of self-confidence because they had been through similar, if not worse, circumstances at some point in their life. It was very reassuring.

After nine months, I finally landed a dream job in risk management at a bank where I had previously applied seventeen times in two and a half years. Read that again. I applied seventeen times in two and a half years. If you think you don't need to send a company another resume because you applied there six months ago and they should already have it on file, think back to this sentence. Once I was on board, as part of a generous benefits package, the bank offers tuition reimbursement. I decided to get my Master of Business Administration, or MBA. Because of the IRS and my employer's policies and limitations on annual tuition reimbursement, I decided to spread my MBA out over four years in order to lower my out of pocket costs. I thought, "Well, four years are going to pass whether I get my MBA or not. Why not go for it, and at the end of four years, have the MBA? I might as well do it."

I remember the day I officially signed up to start my MBA, sitting in a cubicle in downtown Atlanta and staring at a computer screen as if I was starting into the mouth of a lion. It was a nerve-racking day. My previous academic prowess has been well documented above, and I was worried it would be more than I could handle. Could I really pull this off? Was I going to embarrass myself? Could I really focus on a job as well as study for four years?

I had just gotten two kids into college, and downsized to a small town. Life is supposed to be getting easier, not harder. How would I explain this failure?

The best thing I did was to tell everybody I was doing it, so I couldn't quit. It gave me accountability. I talked about it so much that my daughters now reflexively roll their eyes when I bring it up.

My MBA was all online for working professionals through Bellevue University in Bellevue, Nebraska, just outside of Omaha. The school was very accommodating for people going back to school. The professors kept assignments on a weekly schedule so you couldn't find yourself three weeks behind. There were a lot of Saturday mornings working on Excel spreadsheets, reading annual reports, and taking tests while my friends enjoyed leisurely weekends off. It made me realize that the high achievers I know now spent a lot of time working and sacrificing when I had previously been playing.

The first class was Business Performance Management, which meant we jumped right into accounting.

That was my kryptonite in my undergraduate program. It was so boring. Luckily, I had now been working in and around banking for twenty years and was very familiar with Microsoft Excel. We didn't have software like that back in 1982. We also didn't have YouTube and Google. Studying for hours has never been my strength, but I was now able to rely on YouTube and Google to help me through my accounting classes. Concepts that were impossible for me to understand on the pages of the textbook could come alive on a YouTube video in a way that captured my attention and helped me to understand the principles and assignments.

When my classes required us to read books other than textbooks, I would buy both the physical book and the audiobook when possible. I could sit outside with earbuds in, listening to the audiobook and following along with the physical book. It was good reinforcement for me to both see and hear the material. The audio version would often highlight different words in the sentence than I would, to give it a slightly different meaning. I never checked to see if the accounting textbooks had audio versions, but I imagine that would have been worse than a root canal.

At the time, my job required me to commute to Atlanta two days per week, which took about an hour and a half in each direction. I drove about sixty minutes until I got to a bus stop, and then took an express bus the remaining distance. I used that time coming and going on the bus to study for thirty minutes, and I found that it kept me on track and didn't overwhelm me.

I wanted to quit every Monday morning for four years – every single one. There wasn't a week that I didn't want to quit, but I didn't. I kept at it week by week, and it was a wonderful experience. People asked me why I was doing this at my age. I said, "For self-confidence." I didn't want to be unemployed without a master's degree again. I didn't want that 2.7 GPA haunting me anymore. I knew I could do better for myself.

The biggest professional take away from my MBA is that I learned what information is out there. I may not remember all the statistics and accounting formulas, but I know enough to be able to communicate effectively with the people who do. I know how to define problems and who to consult and hire in order to solve them. You have to know that a formula even exists so you know how to Google it. You have to understand the skill sets of other people in your company before you can use them effectively. I am not an expert by any means, but I have learned how to be a more effective communicator and leader.

An important personal take away from my twelve classes is that I learned a lot about diversity. We had a twelve-week class on diversity that covered male privilege, white privilege, prejudices, age discrimination, disabilities, sexual orientation, physical appearance, religion, and even military experience. As someone who went to college in the early 1980s, I never had formal discussions on these topics. It was a truly valuable experience and contributed greatly to my personal growth.

I volunteer with the Children's Ministry at my church. I told my elementary school aged children that I was fifty-eight and in eighteenth grade. I told them about my last first day of school. They don't understand what an MBA is, or even what age fifty-eight is, but I want them to know that you can always go back and chase a dream. It's okay to be a work in progress. That's my hope for them and my hope for you.

Side note: Many people asked me what my major was, to which the answer is Master of Business Administration. At this school it is six accounting classes, two statistics classes, and one class each in negotiation, marketing, management, and human resources.

I can show you where I was standing in my living room in late May 2020, when I got the email notification that our last group project had been submitted. I had already turned in the course evaluation and the degree evaluation. There was truly no more homework or assignments to complete. The feeling was overwhelming. A huge weight was lifted off my shoulders. I paced the floor for ten minutes drinking a Budweiser and drinking in the feeling of accomplishment. I did it. They can't take this away from me. Just thinking back on that moment brings a smile to my face. I know you have memories like that. Sometimes it can just be the way someone says your name, a smell, the right song on the radio, and BOOM, you are back living and dwelling in that success. I hope you go there often.

Now you've heard my story. Tell me your story.

www.MBAat58.com.

Chapter 2

The Popcorn Theory

Not every kernel pops at the same time. When you put a bag of popcorn in the microwave and set the timer for two minutes. They don't all pop at the same time. Some of those kernels start popping at thirty seconds, some pop at forty-five seconds, some pop at a minute, some at a minute and fifteen. Then you've got a minute and thirty, with some of these kernels still popping. Now, had you looked in that bag of popcorn before you turned it on, all of those kernels would look the same. Why don't they all pop at the same time? It's just not their time. Some take a little extra cooking.

If your kids don't go straight into college right out of high school, maybe they're going to pop at a different time. Do you have a new employee that figured out software A pretty quickly, but struggled with Software B? Popcorn. Have a prospect that understood your company's value proposition the first time they saw the demo? Thirty-second popcorn. Next prospect, same demo, don't get it. Two demos later, they start coming around – a minute and thirty popcorn. Could they both be twenty-year customers and refer several customers? Yes. You'll read the story of Dr. Wes who met his wife and married her within ten months. Meet the boy/girl of your dreams but don't start dating for three years? This could be the back story of a fiftieth wedding anniversary. Some popcorn, employees, and prospects don't ever pop. Not a good fit. Cut your losses and move on. Think of that the next time you microwave a bag of popcorn. When you open the bag of popcorn, and you pour it into a bowl, the popcorn that popped at thirty seconds and the popcorn that popped at a minute and a half taste the same. It's all good popcorn.

If you are content with where you are, then simply be happy and content. I'm not suggesting you have to be discouraged with how things turned out. We're all where we are at this point in our lives. Maybe you want to upgrade a portion of your life. Just because you didn't do it at twenty-four doesn't mean you can't do it at thirty-four, fifty-four, or seventy-four. Some seasons of life take a little more time than others. Grow where you are planted.

Chapter 3

The 6 Stages of
Behavior Change

D o you want to lose weight? Do you want to get a new job? Do
you want to finish a degree? Want to start a new business? Is
it going to be someday, or is today day one? Your choice: someday,
or day one. What's it going to take? What's it going to be: someday,
or day one?

How do you take step one? A google search on "how do you
change behavior" yielded an article by Harvard Health Publishing.
The same Harvard you and I think of when we hear the name. I
also found a similar article by Very Well Mind, which is a part of
the Dot Dash publishing family. Their respective references are:

https://www.health.harvard.edu/mind-and-mood/
why-behavior-change-is-hard-and-why-you-should-keep-trying

https://www.verywellmind.com/the-stages-of-change-2794868

In summary, they both agree there are six stages to changing
behavior. It is a process, not an event. You will struggle, and you
may cuss the whole experience. You can expect set-backs and
relapses are all normal. Isn't it nice to hear that everyday failures
and set-backs are normal?! The six stages include:

1. Precontemplation

2. Contemplation
3. Preparation
4. Action
5. Maintenance
6. Relapse

Precontemplation is where you are not even acknowledging you want to change. I've been on six different diets in the last twenty years, I'm not doing another one. I come from a big family, and it's just the way I'm built.

Nobody in my family has ever attended college, let alone graduate from one. We're not classroom kind of people.

My dad was a painter. His two brothers were painters. I've got six cousins that are painters. Ever since I was in seventh grade, I figured I would be a painter. After I flunked the tenth grade for the third time and my little sister caught up with me in school, I dropped out and became a painter. (True story – but not in this book).

Contemplation is where I had the thoughts of "Can I really do this? Can I stick out three-four years, and get an MBA at my age? How am I going to explain this failure to my family and friends?"

This stage is where you weigh the pros and cons of your conflicted emotions. This stage can last weeks, months and even years. In my case, I had never heard of Bellevue University in Bellevue, Nebraska, so I was wondering if it was even a real school. How big is it? Is it accredited? What conference is it in? What classes would I have to take?

You can see why many people get stuck here.

Preparation is where you make a plan of action. This is where I looked at my weekly calendar and decided which days I could study. Where I was going to find the time and discipline to complete this goal. What if I just read fifteen minutes a day at lunch – that would be a good start on my weekly assignment. Would I give up my tennis league on Saturday morning to read annual reports?

If you are considering losing weight, you might eat a salad for lunch and walk for fifteen minutes. How did that feel? Can I do that four days per week? Should I get some better shoes? Let's do some online research for key features of walking shoes. Are there some magazines or blogs for better nutrition? I've been told that I don't have to eat less, I just need to eat better. What does that mean? Do I really have to keep a food journal of everything I eat? How does that work?

Action is where the rubber meets the road. You sign the contract. In my case, I signed up for school, paid an application fee, and forwarded my undergraduate transcripts to get accepted. Some people fail at this stage, because they did not adequately complete the first three stages. Don't do that. It is healthy, wealthy and wise to consider the pros and cons of your new upgrade. Don't apologize if the first three stages take you six months or two years. It will give you a better chance of success because you have researched where your relapses could occur.

During my action phase, I told coworkers, family and friends that I had just signed up to get my MBA. This gave me accountability and a support group.

It is important during this stage to reward your successes. When you complete a class – go out to dinner. Lose five pounds – get a massage. Start a new business and you just landed your first client – do the happy dance in your house. Just land a job in the company or industry of your dreams – get a new outfit.

Maintenance is where you develop the coping strategies for temptation. Sitting in my house and looking at the lake while studying statistics sucked. I wanted to "take a break" and go do something fun. I learned that I needed to study in a different room, so I didn't see the fun I was missing. When I got tired of reading the textbook or listening to my professor, I would search YouTube for other explanations of the same concept. I would set the alarm on my phone for thirty minutes so I knew I had a goal line to get up, move around and let my mind wander.

Relapse is normal. Don't give up. Feel frustrated and disappointed, but DON'T GIVE UP. Go back to the preparation stage and review your action plan. Document your temptations that guided you off the desired path and design some alternatives. Remind yourself how much you enjoyed the reward of your success in the previous step. Go Google the menu for the restaurant where you had that previous success-affirming dinner, and pick out what you'll have the next time. Go get those walking shoes on and walk three mailboxes and back. Get a win, no matter how small. Get back on track.

Chapter 4

Takiya

My name is Takiya, and I'm a licensed Physical Therapist. Physical therapy is a three-year doctorate program following an undergraduate bachelor's degree. I'm proud to say that not only was I the first in my family to earn a doctorate, I was the first to attend a four-year college.

My father dropped out of school in middle school, and became a father at the age of sixteen. My mother was a licensed practical nurse (LPN) who worked in a nursing home. My mother made most of the money for the household. My father worked as a custodian, but he was also a pastor. He started preaching when I was in middle school. His congregation was small, and he didn't have a diploma or any further education, so he didn't draw the kind of income I always thought pastors deserved. What I remember most about him is his work ethic. He worked hard. I never knew about my parents' finances, but I never had to worry because if we needed something, my father would find it – whether it was by working extra, or asking his congregation for help. My parents taught me how to love God and live right. They made sure I had my priorities right.

I had three half-siblings from my father, who were all much older than me. My youngest brother is fourteen years older than

I am, so I was basically raised as an only child. Most would say that only children are spoiled, but I definitely had boundaries. My oldest brother got an associate's degree a few years ago. He now owns his own business, Bo's Trucking Company, named in honor of my grandfather. My sister and youngest brother did not get post-secondary degrees. My sister works for Starbucks factory, and my brother works for the county. I became the first and only one of my siblings to get my bachelor's degree.

My teachers were encouraging and were complimentary of my academic performance, but I did talk too much. That was always noted on my progress reports. My parents expected a lot of me because of how they raised me. I was always in advanced classes, which surprised people because I came from a family without a lot of formal education.

In seventh grade, my family started facing health problems. My paternal uncle was diagnosed with lung cancer, and my paternal grandfather and maternal grandmother both became very ill. We spent a lot of time in the hospitals. Sometimes we would visit the hospital and see one relative on one floor, and the other two on another floor. As stressful as that time was, it helped me to realize that I wanted to help care for people. My parents have a memory book of me with pictures from each grade, and what I wanted to do for my career at each age. In seventh grade, I actually wanted to be a physical therapist! Within the next one-two years, we lost both my uncle and my grandfather. I lost a little bit of my drive because the loss was so difficult. We did everything we could to help, and they still died.

When I was fifteen, our house was becoming difficult to live in. My parents are selfless, and they will always help another person before they help themselves. I moved in with my grandmother, who lived less than a mile up the road. This worked out well for both of us because she had become a widow and my uncle had died, leaving her alone. She got company and I got a better functioning house. To this day, I have not seen the inside of my parents' house. My siblings say it's because they're trying to protect me because it really is that bad. But they will help anyone in need, even when their own house is falling apart. I saw how much they sacrificed, and I wanted to be a success for my family.

I decided to do that by going to college. I didn't know much about college, and I especially didn't know how to pay for it. I could have gone to various universities because of my competitive GPA and SAT/ACT scores, but I ended up going to Armstrong Atlantic State University in Savannah, GA, for my undergraduate degree. As I had not been that far away from home before, I was nervous about moving two and a half hours away. However, I was comforted and reminded of family members who lived in Savannah. Thankfully, I was able to complete undergraduate school with financial assistance provided through scholarships to include the Hope Scholarship, and additional scholarships provided by the university based on good academic standing. When I first got there, I thought physical therapy required a master's degree. They informed me that it was, in fact, a doctoral degree, and I became intimidated. It was only one more year, but at the time it felt like a lot. Once again, I had no idea how I was going to pay for it. I hesitated, but decided to chase my dream.

When it came time to apply to graduate school, I wanted to stay at Armstrong Atlantic. I had great friends, a great church family, and things were going well. It felt natural. My future was planned. But when I went to the PT school interview, I was so nervous. Everything about that interview was horrible. My stockings tore. I was so nervous and I stuttered so much. It was a five-hour interview, and every second was horrible. When I got my rejection letter, I was crushed.

For the longest time, in my waiting period, I really thought that "no" was going to be the end. I didn't see a way for myself after that. I didn't have a plan B, to be honest. I had just focused on that school being my Plan A, and we were going with it. I didn't want to go anywhere else. That "no" actually changed a lot for my life because that "no" allowed me to seek other options. So, I went to Georgia Health Sciences University (now Augusta University) in Augusta, GA, for an interview. Afterwards, I had lunch with my paternal grandmother and my dad and they told me they felt confident that I was going to get accepted to that program.

I had a December 2012 graduation from Armstrong, which would have set me up well to start the PT program in May. Graduation night, everybody wanted to let loose and have fun. But that day I got a letter from Georgia Health Sciences University (GHSU) saying that I was on the waitlist. Now Plan B was no longer in sight, and so I cried, and I cried, and I cried. I had a best friend from my hometown who was actually there with me. She was the best person there for me. She prayed with me; she encouraged me; she stayed with me. That night I just couldn't believe it.

In high school and through college, I had worked as a physical therapist aide (PTA). One day after receiving my waitlist letter I was at work, working hard. I received a phone call from someone at GHSU asking if I had turned in my paperwork yet. Even if you're waitlisted, they send a form asking you to confirm that you'll accept if the space is available. The lady from GHSU called and told me to get that form in because people were dropping out and spots were opening up. It wasn't even a week later, maybe the end of that week, that I got an acceptance letter to GHSU.

The first year of PT school was so hard. There were moments where I really didn't know if I was going to be able to make it. It was so much work, and it was so different from even undergraduate school, and definitely different from high school, where things came easily for me. I didn't have to study as much then, but in PT school, I had to take notes. I had to read deeper; I had to study deeper. It was a strain on me emotionally, physically, and I would say, spiritually. Although, I think in the end, it strengthened me spiritually because I had to rely on God to get me through the program.

In my second year of PT school, my maternal grandmother had a stroke. In that moment I was tempted to give up. But the last words she spoke to me when she was still able to speak were "Don't give up. Don't stop going, and don't let those little boys fool you." That's what she always said whenever I left her. I remember her saying that the last night I saw her verbal and conscious. Looking back, it's fortunate that I was rejected by my top choice PT school at Armstrong. Because I was in Augusta and not in Savannah, I was able to be there for her before she passed. Even in the moments when she was on palliative care at the hospital, they allowed us to sleep in her room, and my professors were so amazing. They allowed me to stay at the hospital. They allowed me to miss class. They allowed me to catch up on work, whether it was tests or work in the classroom. They were just amazing in that capacity, and it was a reminder to me that I had to keep going, that I couldn't stop, that the dream that my family had for me still had to live. Although, it was an obstacle – there were days I had to walk out of the classroom to collect myself, especially when we were learning about strokes – I decided I still had to press through.

I've been a licensed physical therapist since 2016. The wins have been incredible. I've seen so many people be impacted; not by me, but by the spirit of the Lord through me, just helping and encouraging people. A lot of times what I do is more than physical therapy; it's psychological and spiritual therapy as well. I've learned that the wins don't necessarily come from how much money you make or how much vacation time you have, but the countless hours that go into helping and encouraging people.

That's where I've found most of my wins: those times where I was on a schedule, but I got off schedule because I needed to stay in the room and talk to someone to encourage them. When they walked out, they felt better physically, spiritually, and emotionally. It's a holistic approach.

I sometimes have epiphany moments, like "Takiya, you're actually here." I reached my goal and I made my family proud. What I want to pass along to the readers is that I am Takiya G. I'm a thirty-year-old living in the time of so much separation and just a lot of things that I never thought I would see, but I want to say that I don't look at that and say, "That's who I am." I look at it and say, "We shall all persevere through this." I want to pass along to you that even if you are a first-generation graduate, even if you feel like you're not going to make it, that you will. Even if you feel like you don't have what it takes, you definitely do, because the first person to encourage you is yourself, or it should be yourself. I've always heard this: that you are your worst critic. I feel like I could definitely attest to that, but just remember that even when it gets hard, even when it gets tough, that you can make it through. There's always going to be someone who the Lord places in your life to encourage you, to help you through the moments that you feel are the hardest.

Chapter 5

Dr. Wes

'm a dermatopathologist, which means I'm a doctor that looks at skin biopsies under the microscope. When a dermatologist or other caregiver sees something suspicious, or if there is an unusual skin condition, they biopsy it and send it to me. I help make the final diagnosis, and the dermatologist treats the patient based upon my diagnosis and recommendations. Most people become doctors by doing exceptionally well in high school and college and going straight into medical school, eventually finishing training sometime in their early thirties. I, however, took a more "non-traditional" route.

I grew up in a small neighborhood in Valdosta, where I stayed busy playing baseball, basketball, and football. My athletic career vanished at age fourteen, when I discovered girls and other recreational entertainment. My dad worked for Valdosta Cigar and Tobacco Company as a salesman, calling on Mom-and-Pop stores until I was in the sixth grade. Then, he bought a gas station, Sing Oil Company. That's where I grew up, basically. He worked every day from 6:00 in the morning until 9:00 or 10:00 at night for the first four or five years that we owned the gas station. That meant all the kids worked there too, when we got old enough. Most of our time was consumed with school and the gas station, but I did find time to have a little too much fun.

Sing Oil Company was a tire repair, auto repair, and a full-service gas station. My days there were spent pumping gas, washing windshields, checking oil, and doing repair work on truck tires and car tires. If you see an automobile or a tractor-trailer or a front-end loader – anything with wheels on it – I've probably changed that tire before. We had a service truck, and we would go out on the road, mostly helping commercial accounts of ours with flats or blowouts on the highway. A few concrete companies were big customers of ours, so we would change all their mixer-truck tires. I learned how to work hard early, and I think it set a strong foundation for my future.

Hard work was important to us. We were in South Georgia, and there were a lot of people who we felt were unwilling to work for their money. I learned early on that we judged people by whether or not they were willing to work. If you're lazy and not willing to work hard for what you want, then I've got no use for you, regardless of color or socioeconomic status. We had black friends, white friends, Jewish friends. We didn't care, as long as you had a solid work ethic and you paid your bills. We had a lot of personal credit accounts at the gas station. One of my dad's lines that stuck with me all my life, for example if somebody would cheat him out of a $40 gas bill, he would say, "You know what? If they can live with it, I can damn sure live without it."

Despite my indoctrination in the importance of hard work, I didn't have a ton of ambition. Aside from working hard at the gas station, my parents' expectations for me were minimal. They were glad I decided to go to college. I imagine that was probably because my high school performance didn't exactly inspire confidence. I partied pretty hard in high school and college, and was lucky to graduate from either.

I graduated from Valdosta State with a 3.2 grade-point average, and decided I wanted to go to medical school. I was home one day watching a football game with my younger brother and my dad. I was studying for the Medical College Admissions Test (MCAT) when I saw a commercial for flying in the Navy. There were jets taking off from an aircraft carrier. I looked at my brother and my dad and said, "That looks pretty cool right there." At the time, I was driving back and forth to the Kaplan center in Tallahassee to study for the MCAT, and that drive took me right past a Navy recruiting station. I stopped in at the Navy recruiting station a few days after seeing the commercial on TV, told a recruiter that I wanted to fly in the Navy, and asked what the next steps were. He said, "Well, you enlist right here, I'll sign you up, and then, when you get to boot camp, you tell them what you want to do, and they'll steer you in that direction."

I enlisted, as he had suggested. I was at the Navy indoctrination center standing in line to enlist in the Navy, when a lieutenant commander looked at a sheet on his clipboard. He looked at us, and he asked which one of us was Wesley.

I said, "That's me."

He said, "Come here, son. What are you doing?"

I told him that I wanted to fly in the Navy, and this is what the recruiter told me to do. It turned out that I was just a dumbass country boy from Valdosta, Georgia, and I was following directions given by a less than honorable recruiter.

He asked, "You're a college graduate?"

I said, "Yes, sir."

He replied, "Well, come with me."

He took me to a classroom, handed me an aptitude test, and told me to do my best. It consisted mostly of science and aviation-type questions such as determining the angle of ascent or direction of the plane based upon an image of the horizon and the airplane dashboard. I must have done pretty well on it, because after they graded it, he said, "Okay, I'm going to un-enlist you from the Navy today, and you're going to take this paperwork home with you. Does your dad know any state representatives or anything?"

I said, "Yes, sir. I'm sure he does."

He said, "Well, get a letter of recommendation from one of them, fill out this paperwork, and we'll see you at Aviation Officers Candidate School next year."

He sent me home, and I stopped studying for the MCAT because I knew I was going into the Navy. Six months later, I started Aviation Officers Candidate School in Pensacola, Florida.

Every successful person that I know has three or four people in their lives that made significant differences. This chapter of my life introduced me to two of them. The first was the officer that pulled me aside and sent me to Officer Candidate School. The second was Joe, a classmate of mine in Officers Candidate School. One night, we went out in Pensacola, and he saw a girl across the bar that was a little sister in his fraternity. He had not seen her for a couple of years, so he went over to say hello and catch up with her. Being a good wingman, I went over with him. She was there with her younger sister, Marty. Marty and I were just standing there while they were talking, so I asked her to dance. We were married ten months later.

I enjoyed my time in the Navy, but I kept thinking about medical school. I decided I could be a flight surgeon and have the Navy put me through medical school. I had started to look into that process, when my life changed again. My squadron and I had just gotten back from a ten-month Navy deployment on an aircraft carrier where most of us managed to gain about ten-fifteen pounds. We were playing a lot of basketball to lose the weight, and at first, I thought I was crushing it. I was losing weight faster than anyone else. Then I started realizing my vision was a little blurry, I was tired all the time, and I had to urinate four or five times a night. I went to the doctor and told him I thought I was diabetic. He looked at me and said, "There's no way you're diabetic. Get the hell out of here."

I told him my symptoms, and he said, "Well, we'll draw some blood. I don't think it's anything. You've probably just got a virus or something."

A few days later I had to fly to Northern California. While I was in the air, my executive officer radioed and said, "When the airplane lands, go straight to the hospital."

I asked if I could come home first, which was San Diego at the time, but they wouldn't let me. So, upon our arrival, I went straight to the tiny little six-bed hospital in Lemoore, California. My wife had to drive up from San Diego to stay with me. It was there that I received my diagnoses of Type 1 diabetes.

Type 1 diabetes means my body doesn't make insulin, so I can't regulate my blood sugar. Insulin is like a ticket that allows sugar to get inside your body's cells so it can be used to make energy. I was tired, and losing weight because my body wasn't getting the sugar it needed – it was still circulating in my bloodstream. The high sugar was being excreted by my kidneys, and causing me to urinate extra and become dehydrated. High blood sugar can make me feel sick, but the most immediate danger in Type 1 diabetes is that if I take insulin and my blood sugar gets too low, it can become life threatening. When my blood sugar drops, I get pale, sweaty, and jittery. If it stays low, I can pass out, have seizures, or even die.

It's a big adjustment to have to constantly monitor your blood sugar, even for someone with an interest in medicine. It took a lot of education and practice to effectively manage my medications and adjust to a very different lifestyle. Fortunately, they took great care of me in Lemoore, and gave me great instructions. It ended up being a good thing that I was there, and not at a larger naval hospital.

I thought the Navy would reassign me, considering they had probably spent a few million dollars training me. I thought for sure they would send me back to Pensacola to teach in flight school or something, but instead, they declared me unfit for military service and sent me home. It wasn't all bad – I got forty percent retirement pay – but it did feel like I hit a brick wall. We were happy in the Navy. The months at sea were hard, but we had wonderful friends, and we were happy. I didn't have a backup career plan. I applied for a few jobs, but didn't find anything I wanted to do. Marty and I decided to return to Valdosta and take over my parents' gas station.

A few years into working at the gas station, my doctor told me he was retiring. He referred me to someone else, a family practice doctor that I recognized as a guy I had gone to college with. I felt like I had been smarter and better communicating with people than this guy. Now, he was a doctor and I was working at a gas station. I called Marty that day, and said, "I think I'm going to take a couple of months off to study for the MCAT and try to go to medical school." I was 28 years old. She said, "Okay," so that's what I did.

I graduated from Valdosta State in December of '82, and nine years later, in August of '91, I started medical school.

In addition to managing my diabetes, I was also married with two small children in Med School. My focus, along with doing as well as possible in school, was entirely on them. Marty and I missed many social outings with friends and colleagues, but we were quite happy with the sacrifice. My grades suffered some, but I managed to graduate in the middle of my class. During my Pathology residency, the hours were much more reasonable, averaging less than sixty hours per week, and the nights and weekends were dedicated to family if I was not on call.

The most difficult adjustment for me as a diabetic in med school was during the third and fourth years. These are the years in which we spent our time in the hospital caring for patients. We had many different rotations which were aimed at exposing us to the different specialties. We would obviously learn medical care for the patients, but we also learned about these specialties in order to make a decision about which field best suited our goals. During the third year, I had many rotations which involved staying awake twenty hours or more for several days at a time. The long hours and incredibly busy schedule made it a challenge to maintain proper control of my blood glucose levels. I have always tried not to use my diabetes as an excuse not to do what is expected or required, so this was a challenge. I probably averaged checking my blood sugar six-seven times daily, and it was always certain I would have candy or some form of carbohydrates nearby.

A big challenge was to find a career that interested me, but was also diabetic friendly, with regular work hours and a stable environment. In medicine, this significantly limits your choices. Surgical fields were out, as some surgeries can take twelve hours.

In my first year of medical school, I met another person who changed my life. A pathology resident, also named Wesley, was giving us a tour of the hospital and the pathology lab. About half-way through the tour, he glanced at my nametag, which displayed my first name, Robert. He asked, "Do you have a brother named Wesley? I went to college with a guy named Wesley W. Are you related to him?"

I said "Well, that's me." We realized we had taken classes together. Meeting Wesley on that tour is what got me interested in pathology – I had a friend in the pathology department. I saw Wesley several times during Medical School, and he introduced me to the people I needed to know to build a network and gain more experience in the department. Four years after I ran into him on that tour, I started my residency in pathology.

One day in my pathology residency, I was working with one of the teaching physicians (called "attendings") named Omar. Omar was the fourth key influential person in my life. He was a dermato-pathologist from Bolivia, and he was brilliant. One day he was look-ing at a biopsy, when he got so excited I thought he was about to wet his pants. It turns out, the biopsy showed a rare malignant glomus tumor. There had only been about a hundred of these tumors ever reported in the entire world. He said, "Oh, my God, we've got to write this up."

Writing up a case report requires doing a thorough review of all the scientific literature available on a topic, summarizing your particular case, and educating others in the field about your find-ings. None of this is exceptionally difficult for a medical doctor, but it does take a lot of time.

So, I wrote it up. I didn't ask him about it, I just did it. I brought it in a few weeks later, and he was so impressed that I had taken the initiative to do it. From that point forward, he loved me – I mean, viscerally loved me. He helped me get into dermatopathology. He introduced me to Dr. C at University of Texas Southwestern, where I did my fellowship training. Dr. C wanted me to join the faculty with him, but I wanted to return to Georgia. He introduced me to the CEO of AmeriPath. I met with a man, and I'm not sure why, but within thirty minutes of talking to me, he said, "Well, Wes, I'll tell you what we are going to do. We're going to build you a lab in Atlanta, Georgia. You can go talk to the rest of these people and get a feeling for the company, but we'll build you a lab in Atlanta, Georgia, and we'll give you the southeast market. Let's see what you can do with it."

I said, "Yes, sir."

I talked to Marty, and said, "Okay, I've got six other job offers at hospitals and private practice groups, but I have a $500-million company that wants to get behind me and help me start my own lab in Atlanta. I think we should do that." So we did.

I was the only physician for the first six years, so time off was scarce. There were several family trips which involved me bringing a microscope and reviewing cases that were shipped to me while on vacation. We managed to have a pretty normal and loving family, but there was definitely sacrifice by all members of the family.

I was with that company until 2010, when I left and started my own lab in Atlanta. Fortunately, almost all of my clients followed me. Probably ninety-five percent of them came with me because of my people skills, even more than for work ethic. I did work hard, though. I always joke that I used to wake up every morning afraid that my referring dermatologists were going to realize there were many, much smarter folks that they could be sending their biopsies to. I've had that fear my entire career, basically, that they're going to realize that I'm just a dumbass country boy. If you shake a tree, it is likely there's a smarter dermatopathologist that might fall out of it.

Opening my own lab was a leap of faith in itself. Marty and I invested every penny of our life savings into the lab. I have often remarked how fortunate I was to have Marty by my side, because she never vocalized any fear or doubt about the likelihood of our success. This is true for the period from the time I decided to apply to med school, throughout my entire career, and I am certain I would never have succeeded at this level without Marty by my side.

Medicine is a long road. I was forty when I finished all my training and started actually working for a living as a doctor. I completed four years of medical school, five years of residency, and then two one-year fellowships – seven years after medical school, eleven years after college. The light at the end of the tunnel was a career in medicine, and that's what kept me going. Medical school and residency involved a lot of long days, early mornings, late nights, and hard work. My children's pediatrician once told me, "It's not going to be like this your whole life, so just keep your eye on the end. Also, remember to enjoy the journey." And he was right.

I have been more successful than I ever could have imagined. None of this could have been possible if I had limited myself to my childhood goal of being able to join the Valdosta Country Club. I may have taken an extra-long road, but that road was scenic and wonderful, and I would not change a single step of it.

Chapter 6

Sarah

Most of the stories in this book are told from a first-person perspective with them just telling their story (from an outline I prepared) and we edited it down to the version you see here. Sarah, James, and Christine had a little prodding and I kept those interview questions in here so you'll see where I asked them more questions to clarify a point. People read at different speeds and some may appreciate the interaction during the interview. In Sarah's defense, she had 0 time to prepare for this interview. I had a monthly massage from her for two years because she was in Athens and I would go have lunch with my daughter in college afterward. Sarah and I talked about me going back to college and possibly writing a book. My daughter Rachel graduated a year ago so I cancelled my monthly massage and found Christine near my house. I hadn't seen Sarah in a year and didn't even know her last name – and still don't so I booked a massage and we spent the hour doing this interview.

My name is Sarah. I am thirty-two, and I'm a massage therapist. I have a bachelor's degree in horticulture and organic agriculture that I completed in 2013. I graduated from high school in 2006. I traveled to New Zealand a year after college, and I stayed with ten different farming families. I worked in the botanical gardens in

Christchurch by myself. I went there by myself, and I think that the experience of being my own person in a whole other country, in a whole other hemisphere, definitely brought me to a different level of strength in myself. That was a long time ago, it feels like, but it was definitely an influential experience, just learning to be my own person, learning that I had to set my own everything: my own budget. I didn't have any family to comfort and console me. Everyone I was meeting was a new face, a new person, a new culture, a different country, like I said.

I think that, at the age of twenty-three, after completing college and not really knowing what direction to go in, spending that year in New Zealand was definitely where my strength really started to develop because, before that, I was a really social person and always had friends around me, and I was just part of the gang, part of the group. Yeah, I would say forcing yourself to get out there by yourself without any life vest will definitely force you to learn how to swim. That was a pretty big experience for me.

As far as my childhood goes, I had a great childhood. My parents were really involved. I had a stay-at-home mom. We always had vegetables for dinner. We ate meals at the table together. She was very much about physical activity and doing things as a family, so it was a great childhood. I had a stepdad who was a police officer, and he was also in the Army reserve, so he was a structured, good, moral, devoted man.

I also had a biological father in California that I would spend the summers with, and he was more alternative. He also got his degree later in life using his G.I. Bill, because he was in the Coast Guard. He lived in Humboldt, California, which is known as super "granola." Lots of people smoke pot. Lots of people are open to different lifestyles. I had a very nurturing mother, and then I had a father that was very structured and focused, provided for the family. Then I had another father who didn't really want to have the kids. He just wanted to experience life and personal growth.

I had three very strong parental figures in my life. I think that was a good thing. Like I said, I had a good childhood. I had a lot of support. Then, in my teenage years, I always did well in school. I was not a problem for my parents or anything, but, as I got older, I definitely got into doing drugs. I definitely got into just wanting to be liked, just wanting to be part of the cool kids. I got in trouble, and my mom and stepdad kicked me out. They sent me to my dad's house when I was fifteen or sixteen, maybe. They were like, "Look, we can't deal with her. She's lost her mind. You deal with her."

He was happy to have me because I'd never lived with him before. My brother had already moved in with him. He thought, "They just don't know what they're doing, so I'm going to be the hero in this situation and turn this kid's life around." Well, he didn't do that. I was just more trouble from there. I was cutting class and not caring about school. I started failing and started getting other people to do my work for me. I always had really cute boyfriends, though.

Right, so that happened. Then comes my senior year, and my dad and I aren't getting along. I don't know what I'm going to do, but I know school is going to end, so I'm going to have to figure something out. I've got to go to college, and I know, if I move back in with my parents in Georgia, there's the HOPE Scholarship. My grades had been good up until they fell apart in junior year when I was not paying attention. So, I moved back in with my parents in Georgia my senior year, got my act together, got the grades up, got the HOPE Scholarship, and got into a junior college: University of North Georgia in Watkinsville.

I did my first two years there and got an associate's degree in general studies. I got in with some nicer kids. It got boring. I was a waitress for four years. Then I went on a road trip across the United States with a friend that I had worked with at the movie theater when I was younger. We met back up, were hanging out, and we decided to do a Greyhound bus trip across America and just stay with different friends that we knew at different colleges or people we knew that had moved. That was a cool experience. We just had the backpacks on our backs, and we would get to a place and just start hanging out with people, hearing their stories, doing whatever they were doing, and life was just day by day. That was fun.

That lasted maybe two or three months. I think it was when I graduated from college, so it was in April or May and maybe lasted until the fall because then I started going to the University of Georgia shortly after that, so it was for a summer. I ended up at my brother's house in California, and, along the way, my friend that I was with stopped and stayed in Detroit, where she met her husband, got married, and just left me on this trip. Again, I was alone, but that was before New Zealand.

Anyway, I ended up with my brother and his wife, and they had a child unexpectedly, so he was dealing with growing up, becoming a young father, buying a first house, things like that. That made me reassess and be like, "All right, Sarah, you need to get back on track. You need to go to college. You need to definitely not accidentally have a child." That was definitely a clear indicator for me, because it's expensive. His whole life had to become: No more late nights, make sure you can pay the bills, things like that. I wasn't ready for that; I was only twenty or something.

I came back and went to UGA. I started dating a woman, and we were together for two years. I got really into fitness with her, because her mom was a triathlete marathon runner, and she had been a runner all her life and played soccer. The influences in my life at that time were like, "Fitness is cool, especially for women."

I was like, "Yeah, I want to be like these strong women in my life, so I want to get fit. I can do this," and I had the support of someone that loved me, being like, "Yeah, let's go for a run. Let's ride bikes everywhere." Also, I got a DUI, so I had to ride my bike everywhere, but it could've been the female influences too.

I did well in college. I was active; I was fit. I had friends; we went out. I made good grades. I learned a lot. It was a lot of hands-on work. I realized that I liked being physical and being hands-on. College was a great time. I got a lot of scholarship money, and that helped me get to New Zealand. I had a lot of professors that believed in me, and supported me along the way because I was always a hard worker. My parents were hard workers, so I assumed that's just how you're supposed to be.

A little bit of trouble is okay. It's okay to get in trouble.

I asked her "You graduated from UGA; the University of Georgia"?

I got the degree from UGA. I had broken up with the girlfriend. I was feeling, again, unsure about the next step. Definitely, when I get into something, I'm just in that, and I don't always think about the next thing to come. Then, when the end comes, I'm like, "Uh, what do I do?" But I did get that internship together for New Zealand somehow. They wanted me to come out there, which was surprising to me, but I did. It was awesome. It was beautiful. I did a lot of hiking.

Then, when I got back, I had some friends that I knew from jobs that I had worked at plant nurseries during college, and one of the girls had gotten married and started an organic farm, so I worked at her organic farm for two years, just planting things, weeding things, harvesting things. I spent a lot of time alone, just working alone, because that's just the way farm work can be sometimes. I realized that really wasn't what I liked, to be alone all the time, because it gets boring. It can also get depressing if you just have your own thoughts there all the time. It was hot as hell. Georgia summers, whoo! But the food was good, so that was fun.

After about two years, I was like, "I need something else." I also kept losing my job in the winter because there's just not enough work, and a small farm like that can't afford to keep everybody on. She got me a job at the local organic co-op. Then I worked there for about two years, moved up a couple times, and became assistant to the grocery buyer, so I was checking in all the trucks, unloading all the groceries, working hard. I was working hard and not really super excited about the people that I was surrounded by, because they were real[ly] lazy and not ambitious. They just liked to do drugs and talk about things I didn't care about. I knew that that wasn't my end game.

Then I talked to my sister, who's a massage therapist, and she encouraged me, "Have you ever thought about massage therapy? I know you like to do a physical job. I know you're a healthy person. I know you care about fitness. This could be a path for you."

I was like, "Shoot, yeah, that sounds good. I don't like what I'm doing here, so I might as well try something else." I went to the same massage therapy school that she did. I went there in the mornings, 8:00 to 1:00, Monday to Friday, and then I worked at the grocery store from 3:00 to 9:00, Monday through Friday, and sometimes on the weekends.

Massage therapy school took about six months. I finished that, and I immediately got a job at Massage Envy because that's where my sister had worked. It has been awesome. It has been great to meet so many people, learn so many things, hear so many different views on life. I think it really keeps me well-rounded to be a massage therapist, because it's a lot more listening unless I'm encouraged to talk. It's a lot more listening, usually, because people are here to relieve their stress. People are here to relax and just get their bearings straight again after we all just worked so hard every day. I like being able to be part of that: helping people come back to their peace of mind, their healthy habits, and their focus on self-care.

Sometimes it's a sordid path to get to where you belong, and who knows? I don't know if I'm done yet, but it's important to be open. It's important to listen. I think structure is important. Every day I wake up, and I drink my twelve ounces of water. That's key, because water is crucial to almost all functions in our bodies. Then I hit my workout. I usually work out for one to two hours a day. I break it up by body section: chest and back, biceps and triceps, core and shoulders, and legs. Then I do cardio day two days a week. Even on days when I don't want to do it, I know that if I do it, I will have a better day than if I skip it. For me, I just try to stick with that, care about myself, love myself, so that I can give my best self to my clients. That, overall, makes the world a better place.

If I take care of myself, and I can show somebody else love because I have that space in myself to do that, maybe they can do that [too], and so on and so forth. Then there's less terrible stuff in the world. It's knowing yourself and having structure and goals – I think that is really what gets you on that path to being your best self.

I askedher: "Looking back, what should you have recognized?"

I should have recognized?

I responded: "Bad paths you were on?"

I don't know, Doug. If I didn't take those bad paths, maybe I wouldn't have compassion like I do now. If you never mess up, you think everyone should just never mess up. Looking back, I guess I wish I had ... I don't know. I'll have to come back to that.

What were the turning points?

Turning points sometimes were when I was just living for myself, and I would look back and think about all that my parents had sacrificed for me, the long hours they'd worked, the money that they put into raising me, the time, the love, the care, and the fact that I was just wasting my time and my abilities. Those were always turning points if I would get too far down the paths of drinking too much or just partying with friends and not thinking about the future. Just love – love brings you back. If somebody really shows you a lot of love, then it feels like real crap if you just throw it away and don't appreciate it.

I have a boyfriend now. We've been together for five years, and we just bought a house together two years ago. We don't plan on having kids. We like to travel and go and just enjoy life, so we have two indoor cats. We just enjoy each other. We have a pretty simple, happy life. It's nice. He repairs and restores guitars. He's a craftsman, a woods craftsman. He works with his hands, too. He always has. His father did, too.

Something you would want to pass along to the readers: perseverance, second chances, late-bloomers?

You've got to keep going. Every day, you've got to get up, and you've got to keep going. Every time you cut yourself slack, you are that much further away from your goals, so in order to get where you're going, really feel proud of yourself, and be able to have that space in yourself to give to others, you've got to persevere. You've got to keep going. You've got to set goals and standards, and you've got to hit those marks every day. Then you've got to raise those marks and keep hitting those marks.

Late-bloomers? That's great. Don't ever give up on whatever it is that you want to achieve. It may evolve as time goes on. When I was young, I thought I was going to be a children's book author, but I am definitely not an author of any kind today. You just keep trying. There's something out there that's going to be the right fit for you. I never thought I was going to be a farmer, but that job is very important. I thought I was going to be taller. I didn't think I would be living in the south, but I like it here.

What prejudices was I taught? Well, we definitely went to church when I was young. We were Southern Baptists, so I was taught you have to be saved, you have to not be gay, and you have to not have sex till you're married.

How did your parents respond when you had a girlfriend for two years?

Well, they didn't like it at first, and they just never believed that I was gay, but these days, it's a lot more open-ended, the whole sexuality conversation. Sometimes, when two minds meet, and two levels of physical ability, it's just so stimulating and so fun that that's just who you want to spend all your time with. Maybe it's not as much the romance. It becomes romantic because you love each other so much, and it's so fun to be together, but I think that that's not as understood sometimes with some of the older generations or some of the more religious populations. My boyfriend and I have talked about that too, and he's like, "If you look at tribal populations, they don't promote same-sex couples because that doesn't produce children, so eventually you could end your whole population and heritage."

Typically, there's certain reasons why that may not be the best for the population in general, but I'm just saying, from a meeting-of-the-minds point of view, it can be interesting, man or woman. People are people. I don't know. My ex-girlfriend moved to Texas and got married to someone else, and that was a long time ago. I had several boyfriends after her, but I didn't have any other girlfriends. I did try dating women after her, but it was just her.

So, it was really a meeting of the minds.

Yes.

My siblings are all doing great. My older brother has two children, a wife, and a big house in Riverbank, California, close to San Francisco. He is very handy. He loves building things and fixing things. They have a boat. They go out skiing all the time. They're a fun, happy, healthy family. I love him and look up to him. He's two years older than me.

Then I've got a sister two years younger than me who is the massage therapist with her own private business. She's the one who encouraged me to consider a career in massage therapy. She loves to travel. She loves to hike. They're always going out and hiking. She has a boyfriend, and they both have two big dogs. They're very outdoorsy. She still lives in the same area as me, so we're pretty close.

Then I have a sister four years younger than me who also lives in California, in southern California – San Diego. She is a biologist. She got her degree in biology from UGA with a minor in entomology. She is working in a chemistry lab in San Diego at a university that I don't know the name of, but they're working towards coming up with a Coronavirus vaccine. She just got her promotion this week, actually, where she's working on developing training systems for their staff, so she's really good with communication, leadership, and group development.

How old were you when your parents got a divorce?

I was two, a baby, and then my mother remarried within a year I think, to my stepfather, so I only had a year without a father in the picture.

So those two younger siblings...

Are from my stepfather, so their parents have always been married.

So, you pretty much had a father your whole life except from two to three.

Yes, and even then, I probably saw my father, but they were just going through a divorce, so it might have been a stressful time. I don't really remember.

Then you were fifteen, and kicked out of the house. Right?

Yes, I did. I did. (nodding head & looking down).

Your older brother, where was he living at the time?

If your parents' divorced when you are fourteen or fifteen, I'm not sure exactly when, but the courts give the child the opportunity to choose what parent to live with. He just wanted to see what it was like to live in California versus Georgia, so he moved out there when he was fifteen. He was two years ahead of me in beginning to live with my dad. Then my youngest brother is from my dad and stepmom, and he also lived there, so my dad was raising two boys, my two brothers, when I moved in. They were good kids. They didn't really get in too much trouble.

Were they accepting of their sister?

Yeah, I would say so.

They didn't pick on her?

No. We were social. Everybody was out with their friends. You know what I mean? That was good.

I appreciate that you think my story is important enough to include in your motivational-speaker book. That's generous of you.

Chapter 7

April

'm a thirty-four-year-old physical therapist. Our office works on Doug and those like him who still think they can play tennis and golf like they are twenty-five. I am the director of a physical therapy clinic, and I have a doctorate degree in physical therapy. My family grew up in a tiny little town called Crawfordville, GA, on my parents' dairy farm. I had a brother and two sisters, and since there was only one boy, we were all considered boys, and we worked. We baled hay, milked cows, and did everything my dad did. My mom did, too. She and my dad ran the farm together. Even when we were little, they would wake us up at 4:00 in the morning and take us to the dairy barn. We had pallets on the floor where we slept while they milked the cows. We came back home, got ready for school, and went off. It was definitely working. Everybody helped and contributed to make it all come together.

I went to a very small private school starting at age four because the public school in our area doesn't have a good graduation rate. The majority of kids that go there don't go to college. We went to a little private school, but it was definitely a middle-class kind of place. It wasn't one of those $15,000-a-year schools. It was $3,000 a year, but, for dairy farmers with four children, it was a lot. As a kid, we bought our clothes at Wal-Mart. We did not go on vacations. They paid year-round, monthly payments to send us to school there, so it was a huge sacrifice on my parents' part for their kids.

My parents met in high school and married two years after they graduated. Neither went to college. My mom worked as a teller at a bank, and my dad was on the farm. No college. My dad has one brother who went to college, and my mom had siblings that went to college. But, for them, that just wasn't the route. The expectation was: You're going to work hard and contribute because we're sacrificing a lot for you, so we expect you to be thankful in return by pulling your weight.

My grandmother lived maybe a half-mile down the street. My aunt and uncle lived at the bottom of the hill, and we were at the top of the hill. It was all family property from my great-grandmother and great-grandfather – that was their farm. When they got too old to work it, my dad took it over. It was nice and private. Out in the middle of nowhere, when you're young, you think is the worst place ever to be. Looking back, it was a wonderful place to grow up because we ran free, did whatever we wanted, built forts, and were outside way more than inside.

My siblings always joke that I was the perfect child because I was the one who was the pleaser. Being the third of four, I was laid back and just went with the flow. Whatever my parents said, that's what I did. I always loved school, so I'd come home right from school, sit down, and do my homework because that's what I was supposed to do. Whereas all my siblings were like, "Nah, we'll wait until Mama beats us until we sit down to do it," or my brother, who's a year older, would be like, "Here, just do mine, and I'll pay you five dollars for it." He did that all the way through high school. He was not cut out for school.

My mom loved sports, and she grew up in a house of five kids, so they all played together – basketball and everything – so she raised us outside. We'd play basketball, softball, we'd ride our bikes, run, and just be very active outdoors, so sports was instilled in me. Mom's approach was, "You're going to at least try it. If you hate it, then I'm not going to make you play, but you're going to try athletics because I want to go and watch you play." All of my siblings were very involved in sports. Being at a small private school, you could play every single sport with no problem, so through the summer, you're practicing softball. My brother was in football. As soon as that ended, basketball started, so we'd just transition right into that. Then track would start, and then spring softball and spring football, so it was never ending sports pretty much our whole life, which was good. It taught us teamwork, and to work hard and be a leader. We were all pretty athletic, so I feel like all of my siblings were captains on the teams. A lot of leadership, I think, was built from that. There is a downside of having sports as your identity. If you are not good enough to play college sports, you're lost. You don't know what to do.

All of my siblings and I went to college because that was just expected. Pretty much everybody in my class in high school went to college. It didn't matter what you did, you were just going to go and figure it out. I was the kid at Georgia College in Milledgeville, for two years, with the undecided major. At the end of year two, my advisor demanded, "You have to pick a major right now, today," and I had no idea.

I shrugged my shoulders and said, "I don't know." My advisor sent me to the learning center to take all these tests about your personality and who you are. My test results showed sports and healthcare, sports and healthcare. I didn't want to be a coach because you don't really get to have a life when you're a coach or working in that area. I figured healthcare was the more promising route, could give me more of an outside life, so then I started trying to tie it together.

Actually, a friend of mine had just gotten accepted into athletic training, so I thought, "That could be cool - sports and healthcare right there together." I didn't do much research on it. I just decided, "Hmm, I'll do that." I applied, got in, and that was a program that only had ten people, so I felt like I was back in high school where you're in your tiny little class with ten other people. Expectations were high because it was divided between the classroom and then you had to go out and do clinicals with sports teams. It started to hit with me, "Gosh, I don't have much of a life doing this," because you're in class from 8:00 to 12:00, and then I'd be at a high school or at one of the college sports teams' practices from 1:00 to 4:00 or 5:00, and then we'd do treatments afterwards. I thought, "Well, I like this, but I'm not really involved in sports a whole lot because I'm not getting to play. I'm just sitting here watching people, which isn't that fun."

I did my last clinical, right before I graduated, in Morgan County with their high school doing football. The athletic trainer had been there for twenty-something years. He was the longest high school athletic trainer in the state of Georgia. He got to school at 9:00 in the morning, and he left whenever the last game or practice ended that night. He told me, the prior year, before I got there, he had totaled up his hourly pay, and it was $2.13 an hour. I had that break-down moment: What have I done? I should have been a coach. At least I'd only have one season. This is year-round, every single team.

He told me that day, "If you want a family, don't be an athletic trainer." Well, I was supposed to graduate in three months with an athletic training degree. I was in undergraduate school for five years because of the undecided major for two, and then I decided and had a year to take all the prerequisite classes. At the end of that five years, I'm frustrated and thinking, "There's nothing else you can do with an athletic training degree except be an athletic trainer, and I'm going to make $2.13 an hour working six days a week every day of my life until I'm 150 to be able to pay for everything." There were some bad moments in there: "I have no idea what I'm going to do with my life at this point." I really had no idea, so the more I went with this athletic trainer and hung out with him when I had to go on my clinicals, the more he kept saying, "Just go to physical therapy school; go to PT school."

I was mad at myself and said to him, "But PT school, that's three more years of my life. I've already spent five in undergrad, wasting time. I'm going to be twenty-eight before I get done with college," and my little life plan I had in my head was I'd be married and have kids by then, so a little curveball was thrown. I graduated, had my degree, passed my boards, so I was an athletic trainer, but I started looking for jobs. I moved home with my parents after college because I hadn't found a job. I found one at a tiny little high school that was not known for being a good environment, and they were going to pay me – I think the salary for the year was about $28,000. Thankfully, I didn't have student loans because of HOPE scholarship, so I'd gotten away with that and my parents' help paying for apartments and that kind of thing, but I'm thinking, "$28,000! I can't even afford rent and my bills at that rate."

I moved back in with them, trying to figure out what to do. At the time, I was working at Reynolds Golf Course at one of the golf shops, and Dr. Cowles came in. He just started talking to me that day. "What's your plan? Where do you see yourself in a couple years? Where are you going?"

I felt like an idiot because here's Dr. Cowles, who owns this entire medical complex, and I just graduated college, and I'm like, "I don't know. I don't want to do what I just got a degree in, and I'm not sure." He told me, "There's a physical therapy clinic in my complex. Come be their aide. See if you like it, and if you do, go to physical therapy school." I thought about it for about a week, and I was undecided, "I don't know. Should I do that? I don't have anything to lose. Why not? I'm making $9.00 an hour at the golf shop, so I'll give it a try."

I went and got the aide job at Cowles Clinic, and was overwhelmed with how much it was, because at the time, there was only one physical therapist there, and he was seeing about twenty-four patients a day with just him. I became the exercise girl, and he did hands-on work, and patients were just in and out, in and out, in and out, all day. It was exhausting, but I started to really enjoy watching people get better and seeing their gratitude for what he was able to do for them. The athletic training went along with that, but athletes, a lot of them, especially when they get to the college and pro level, they're not grateful to an athletic trainer because they think they're on this higher level of being, so it's all about them, rather than, "These are the people that support me and get me where I need to be." But, when you just have your average people that just want to play golf or go swim or water ski, they were very thankful to have that quality of life back, and it really influenced me to say, "Okay, I like helping people. I'm caring and compassionate. I think this could be a good field. I'll just apply and see what happens."

So, I did, and I got in, but I dreaded the thought of three more years of school. You sign a contract going in that you will not work because the physical therapy program is very rigorous, and they want full dedication to that. I went to Armstrong Atlantic down in Savannah, which now is called the Armstrong campus of Georgia Southern. It's the only graduate-school program they have on campus, so it was really weird going back to a campus and being part of the old people there. Everybody else is eighteen or nineteen, all excited about college, and we were the old people. You think, "Ah, twenty-four is not old," but, when you look at eighteen to twenty-four, there's a big difference there.

I started back there, and it was really funny. The first day of class, they make you go around the room, introduce yourself, tell what your interests are, where you're from, and all that. We got halfway through, and one of the students was like, "Where's the black girl?"

I said, "What?" It was all white people in our class. "The black girl? What are you talking about?"

"There was a girl named April Jackson on the list. That's got to be a black girl, right?"

I'm like, "What? I'm April Jackson. That's the most racist thing I've ever heard."

She said, "I thought everybody whose name was Jackson was black."

I stated "Haven't you ever heard of Stonewall Jackson, Shoeless Joe Jackson, or any of these people?" No, a Jackson girl is black. So, she went through a little transformation before I started. That was kind of funny.

I lived with a girl in my PT class. They sent out a roster of everybody's names, and it said, "If you want to live together, here's their email and phone number." We just randomly said, "Okay, we'll live together." We met before school started and got our apartment. I started school, and it was definitely very strenuous. From the very first day, you're in class some days from 8:00 to 5:00. Be ready to have tests thrown at you every single week. You get one opportunity to fail a test. You retake it. If you fail again, you're out. You can come back next year if you want to try again. I was terrified going into it because I was a good student, but tests – I always had that test anxiety and would freak out about it, so that terrified me. You only get one chance, really, and it's either sink or swim.

Out of like six hundred applications to our school, they chose twenty, so they put a lot on you because they could have had somebody else, easily, to take your spot, so they expected you to be serious, to give it your all, and to be devoted to it. That was a lot of tuition they're going to lose if they could have gotten somebody else, and you drop out. There were lots of all-night studying days, and spending hours and hours at the library. It wasn't near as fun as undergrad. There was no, "Eh, I'll do it. We'll go party right now, and we'll come back to it." That didn't really happen a whole lot. Being in Savannah, you have to carve out a little time for Tybee Island and downtown, but, during the week, it was schoolwork all the time. It was our job.

Living with someone in your class, you think, "Oh, it would be great. You can help each other study," but your stress levels were at their highest at the exact same times. You're around each other from 8:00 to 5:00 in a classroom, and then you have to come home and be around each other even more. It was tough living – especially girls. We tend to be brattier and mean to each other. Thankfully, it was a two-bedroom, two-bath apartment, so we had our escapes, but there were rough days where we stared at each other, "Get out. Just go away from me. I can't stand to look at you anymore."

We did help. We relied on each other too because, even though we were both stressed to the max, we knew what the other one was going through and could really relate. You had to lean on each other but have your time away from each other too.

I did fail one anatomy test. It was an online test that our professor had given us, and she was one of those people who was a clinical researcher. She'd never laid hands on a single patient. She had dissected probably thousands of bodies, and she was one of those who would try and find new tissue so she could name it. She was a genius. She could tell you anything you wanted to know about the human body, but give her a real patient, and she was terrible. It was online tests from her. I had been home for a baby shower for one of my friends that weekend, got back to Savannah at 6:00 on a Sunday night, and the test was due at 9:00, so I'm frantic. My roommate and two other girls from our class were in the living room watching Hocus Pocus, drinking beers, just hanging out because they had already done their test, and I'm in frantic mode trying to take this test. It ended up that all four of us failed that test.

Then there was the embarrassment that your whole class knows you failed it. Now all the pressure is on. You have to pass this next one, or you're done, and you have a lease for the next six months that your parents have been paying for. It was me, two guys, and then another girl. The other girl never really hung out with any of us; she kept to herself. Me and the two guys, we got together and just studied nonstop for forty-eight hours. We all passed the next time, thank God. There may have been a little help on those online tests. We all three sat there together, and it was different versions of the same test, so it wasn't the same questions, but we pooled our brainpower to make sure none of us got kicked out. After that, I was determined, "Okay, if it's a test weekend, there's no going home. I'm sorry if you're having babies or getting married, friends, but I have to focus here because I can't go enjoy your happiness and then kill my career in the process."

We had clinicals built into our program, where you had to go and do free-labor work so you can learn to treat real patients and see how other therapists work. I did two in Savannah and then one out in Denver, Colorado, which was really fun. I had a friend who was out there in nursing school, and she said, "I've got an apartment. You can sleep in my bed with me. Just come out here, and we'll make it work." She had a boyfriend, so she was never there anyway. I just lived in Denver for about four months and worked in University of Colorado Hospital, which was a really good learning experience just to be around totally different people. That's probably the biggest city I've ever lived in. It was amazing, the translators you had to work with, and Farsi is apparently a very highly spoken language in Denver, which I never would have thought. I really became friends with the Farsi translator because we'd work together three days a week, and he was a young guy from – I can't remember – somewhere in the Middle East. That was his job; he just went around the hospital all day translating for Farsi-speaking patients.

It was neat to be out there, to be surrounded by a totally different atmosphere, and to be out of the south and see how people treated each other. It was even neat to see the prejudices that people automatically thought about me being from the south. They would say, "Oh, a white girl from the south. She doesn't like black people. She loves sweet tea," which I do, but I have many friends who are black. It was funny to hear that – that people just automatically assume, "Oh, you're from the south. You're racist." They didn't know anything about me other than I was white, I was from the south, and that I talk with a southern accent, so it was just automatic.

It was interesting, and my younger sister, she spent a lot of time in Wyoming. She got the same thing out there. People would automatically assume, "Oh, Amanda hates black people because she's from the south." It's like, "What? What do you people learn wherever you're from?" It was interesting just to hear that and to see people's expectations of you before they know anything about you. Hopefully, I taught some of those people that's not how all southerners are. We are friendly, nice people.

Physical Therapy school was definitely the most stressful time of my life. It was hard seeing, at that point in my life, all my friends back home getting married, having babies, doing all this stuff, and here I am. I'm in my mid-to-late twenties, and I'm still in school. It was funny to see their perspective: "Oh, you're living in Savannah, you're single, you're just living the life. I wish I could do that." But I was on the other side, like, "Gosh, y'all are married, and you're settling down and having babies. You're not broke all the time. Why don't I have that life?" I guess the grass is always greener no matter where you're at, even with the good and the bad from every perspective.

With physical therapy, you never really get a master's. You just go straight from your bachelor's to your doctorate. I think the reason they got away with that was PT used to be a master's degree. There was no such thing as a doctorate, but the industry has been trying to get direct access to patients for physical therapists, so we don't have to say, "Go see your doctor, and get a referral, and then come back and see us." With direct access to patients, if somebody calls and says, "My shoulder hurts," you can just say, "Come right to us. We can go ahead and treat you."

The industry changed it to a doctorate because, "If we learn to diagnose and to really be able to isolate and treat what's really the problem without them having to go to a doctor, then we can get direct access," but the American Medical Association said, "Ah, no. We want that doctor's visit. That's a co-pay. That's an office visit. We're not going to be taken out of this circle." Every state has some varying degree of direct access, but they changed the master's to the doctorate. I think it went from a little over a two-year program to a three-year program, so they added that, in your last year, you're pretty much doing clinicals twelve weeks at a time. We learned more of the diagnosing and trouble-shooting, but insurance controls everything in healthcare, so we still don't get the direct access unless people want to pay out of pocket and go around insurance. That's the only way we can really get direct access.

I finished the doctorate degree in Savannah. I had met a guy when I was there who was a lot younger than me. I didn't know he was that much younger, but he was, so he was still in undergrad when I graduated. When I was at the PT clinic doing my aide job, they had offered me, "If you come back and work for our clinic, we'll pay for one semester of tuition." It was a trade-off: "Instead of giving you a sign-on bonus when you graduate, we're just going to pay you upfront," so that way it helps with student loans and that kind of thing. So, I didn't have the stress at graduation of interviewing and trying to figure out what I was doing. I'd already signed with a company, and they said, "Okay, we need you in St. Mary's, Georgia. That's where you're going."

I had no idea where St. Mary's was. It's at the very bottom south of Georgia on the coast – the last exit before you go into Florida on 95. It's about an hour and forty minutes south of Savannah, right at Fernandina Beach, so not a bad place to be thrown to. I got there, and it was a really big clinic. There were eight or nine therapists there. Four of us were straight out of college – so a lot of new blood – and all of us were scared to death and really had no idea what we were doing. We knew, but we were terrified that we didn't, and we just got thrown to the wolves. It was, "Here's your schedule today. You've got ten or twelve patients. Figure it out." Thankfully, one of the new grads and I became friends and clung together, so we helped each other, would bounce ideas off each other, and figure it out because our director was busy doing his own thing and didn't have time to help us. It was just, "Do the best you can. If it doesn't work, then try something different, and you can always send them back to the doctor."

What I found in those first couple of months was it really wasn't how much you knew, or if you could really diagnose the person with exactly what they had. It was connecting with them and getting them to trust whatever you were saying, whether it was right or wrong. If they believed in what you were doing, then they'd buy in. A lot of times, just having somebody put their hands on you and move you makes you feel better. The more you do it, the more you figure it out. "This doesn't feel right, or this is too tight," that kind of a thing. The truth about physical therapy, the best way to learn it, is just by fire. Jump in and figure it out, because you know all the underlying muscles that are there; you know the bones; you know all that stuff has been drilled into your head, so you just figure it out as you go.

After I was there for a little over a year, my boss came to me and said, "There's an opening in Greensboro, GA. We want you to go there." My initial thought was, "No, I like it here. I like being on the coast, and the beach is right here. I've made some friends." I knew, back home, all my friends were married with kids and doing that whole thing. I thought, "I'm not going to have anybody to hang out with because I'm the single girl." Well, I was dating but not married. That went on for a couple months: "We want you to go" and "No, I don't want to" back and forth. They finally were like, "April, you're going to Greensboro. We're sending you home."

I was mentally stomping my foot like a little girl, "Oh, okay, I'll go," which worked out because, right at that time, Cody proposed. His family is from the Atlanta area, so that would be a good in-between location for both of us. He had just graduated with a degree in rehabilitative science, geared up to go to PT school or OT school or something like that, but I knew Augusta is not that far away. It would be doable to live in this area and for him to get a degree in one of those things, so we moved back. My stipulation for moving back was, there was a girl named Leanne who worked at the clinic at that time, and I said, "I want to know that Leanne's going to be there and that she's going to be willing to help me," because it was a totally different patient population. Down there, there's a naval base, so I was working with young, healthy military members. Here, it's mostly Medicare age, the typical weekend warrior. They play golf; they play tennis; but they're not in the best shape. They go to the gym a couple times a week, maybe. It's a totally different patient population, dealing with more degenerative stuff, rather than specific injuries where I was before.

They said, "Oh, yeah, Leanne will be there, and she's a great mentor. You'll learn a lot from her." I got here and, about two months in, Leanne tells me she's moving to Wyoming. I'm rolling my eyes thinking, "Great." At that point, I was trying to decide, "Okay, do I stay here and just suck it up and hope whoever they get to replace her is good, or do I look for a new job?" She was going to be there for another three months before she left, so they were doing some interviewing and trying to figure out who they would get to replace her. I was sitting there one day, and they said to me, "April, we think we want to replace her with you. We want you to be the director." My jaw just hit the floor. I'm like, "What? I'm not even confident treating a patient, and you want me to run a business? They didn't teach us that in PT school." It kept going, and I would politely decline and say, "No, I'm good. I'm just going to be a therapist."

It got to maybe three weeks before she left, and they said, "April, you're the director. If you want to stay at our clinic, you're the director of this clinic, and we're going to get you a new grad to come in, and you can train him." I'm like, "Dear Lord, nobody taught me this." They promised, "Oh, we'll hold your hand. We'll help you through it. It'll be good." Well, I'm six years in, and I'm still waiting for the training and the "holding my hand." It was another trial by fire: "Just do it. These are the reports you need to run. This is how you need to talk to doctors. Go for it, you'll figure it out."

Since I've been here, I've had four therapists, and the problem is, it's a small area. They've brought in a lot of new grads, and young people aren't really attracted to this area because there's not a lot for young people to do. There's the lake, but there's not bars and restaurants and things like that for people to do. It's hard to meet young people unless you've got kids. It was a revolving door for a little while. I felt like I'd get a new grad to a place where I wasn't having to watch their every move, and then they'd be like, "Oh, I'm leaving. See you, April," and it'd start all over again.

But, through those six years, without even realizing it, just being in the area, forming the relationships, we've built a really good business. People know us, and, thankfully, Takiya has now been there for two and a half years. People know her and trust her and have confidence in what she can do. It's gone from, "We need to advertise everywhere and get the name out," to the point where you treat a couple of patients and say, "If you need us, or if your neighbor needs us, let us know." That's what we get. People come in the door and say, "My neighbor told me to come see Takiya," or, "My friend on the golf course said to come see April," and that's how we built our business. Now we really don't advertise at all. It's just all word of mouth, which is a really good thing, but I feel like my struggles are still in the running-a-company part. They don't teach you that at all in my undergrad courses I went through or in PT school.

I never really thought about running a PT clinic, but now that I've been in it, the thought is, "Okay, I'm working my tail off for these other people, and I don't really know what I'm doing, but I guess I'm doing good enough because we're making money. But they're making all this money, and I'm just working all these hours and not getting a whole lot of money." I'm making a good living, but not what they're doing. Futurewise, I'm thinking, "Open your own clinics, reap the benefits of your work rather than letting someone else reap it," but with having a family now and wanting to have more kids, hopefully, it's just not on the forefront right now. That's the future. Hopefully, it's not too far away but maybe one day.

I wish I would have done more research before just jumping into a career. I thought it just sounded neat and athletic training would be cool, and I'm still an athletic trainer. I just don't practice, but I have my license. If I wouldn't have gotten into athletic training, I never would have done PT, so I'm glad I did because it got me to where I think I want to be. I wish I would have been smarter at that point to say, "Okay, this sounds like a neat career for me, but let me do more research and found out exactly what's involved in it."

Then, even with physical therapy, I worked in the clinic, and I knew the guy that I worked for then was really busy, but I didn't see the after-work stuff that he took home – piles of charts to have to type at night. He actually ran that clinic, and he did home health on the side to try and make a little more money because he didn't want to have to work until he was seventy. He wanted to grow his wealth faster and provide more things for his family. I wish I would have looked more into that part of it – not that money is the only thing you should look at, but the hours and the dedication that you have to put into it.

The other part is it can be draining all day to work in a job that, yes, is rewarding, and you help people, but you have to listen to a lot of whining, and you take other people's burdens onto you. It can be mentally exhausting, emotionally exhausting, but, every day, we have to put on our happy face and go in and be nice to everyone. If you're already having a bad day, and you're trying to pretend it's not, and then someone comes in and just unloads on you all their problems, it's like, "I can't handle you today." You learn quickly working with the public that you can meet all kinds of crazy.

I would say ninety-five percent of the people are good, but you get that five percent that are trying to get on disability or that want to sue their job for something. Those are the ones that really drain you.

You think to yourself, "This is not why I got into this field. I want to help people that want to get better." I had a girl in her thirties one day tell me how I could get on disability. I responded, "There's nothing wrong with me," and she said, "That doesn't matter," and it's because there's nothing wrong with her either. She could work, but she has been on disability since she was about twenty-eight. She wanted to have kids, and I said, "You can't work, so you can't provide for your kids," and she said, "The government will pay for it. It'll be fine." Those are the days when you shake your head, "Why do I do this? Why do I put so much of myself into others when they couldn't care less?"

They're the ones you can never get rid of because all their paperwork has to be in order of, "I tried therapy; I tried pain management; I tried all this stuff, and nothing gets me better." You get rid of them, and in two months they're back, saying, "The doctor wanted me to try again," and it's very frustrating.

I think my message to the readers would be: It's okay to not know what you want to do. It's okay to not pick a major right away. I went to college because I was supposed to go to college. That's what everybody did. Then I picked a major because somebody told me, "You have to pick a major TODAY. You've got to decide." Then I turned down a career because someone said, "Don't do this career. You're never going to have a life or a family." It's okay to do it on your own time and to figure it out and just do your research. I think one of the best things is to go and shadow people or do internships or get around the job you're considering because there may be parts of it you never thought about that can sway you towards it or away from it.

The other thing is: I always had this concept in my mind that whatever you pick for your major you have to do for the rest of your life; that's your job. That's not true. You can do anything you want. You can always go back to school. You can go into a completely different field. Don't feel like, when you pick something, that you're headed down this narrow tunnel that you can never get out of. There's more to it, and you write your own story. You can do whatever you want.

Chapter 8

James

'm a twenty-nine-year-old tennis pro at Reynolds Lake Oconee, and I have a bachelor's degree in sports sciences with a focus in sport management. I grew up in Sacramento, California, with my parents, and I had a half-sister who lived with her mom. I went to Natomas Unified School District, which is important for me because it's actually the most diverse school district in the nation as far as demographics go. That was really cool for me because I had a really good childhood. My parents were both there. My parents both worked and had good jobs, but I got to see a lot of other people who didn't quite get that opportunity.

I saw a lot of my friends whose parents were either illegal immigrants, or on drugs, or their parents were not there. For the most part, that was a lot of my friends, so I got to live the good, sheltered kind of life, but at the same time, I got to gain the appreciation for it just from seeing my friends and everybody else around. I think that was really big in what shaped me. I grew up, obviously, playing tennis and swimming.

My mom was huge into having me watch the old Dickens movies. We were big into Charles Dickens, so we'd watch different versions of *A Christmas Carol*, *David Copperfield*, and *Great*

Expectations and things like that. We'd always sit down and either watch a new version that would come on, or we would read them. I would say my home life was pretty calm, very structured, and healthy. I was very, very, very hyper growing up, though. In elementary school, I was hyper to the point where I was an annoying kid.

In fourth grade, I was getting in trouble in school because I was too hyper. It made conflicts with other kids and stuff like that, so then I got diagnosed with ADHD, which is something I'm happy about. I think it's a good thing to have because it means that your brain is pretty active. I've had some people work on me with that and how to make myself calm and focused a bit more, so that was definitely very helpful for my life.

Moving forward into middle school and high school, I did lots of tennis and swimming, then I got into track and wrestling, mock trial, skiing, and snowboarding. I was able to find a lot of outlets to get my energy out, which was very good and helped me become more of a well-rounded person in my opinion. My mom got her journalism degree from Sacramento State, and then she had me. My dad actually went to University of the Pacific, where I went, but he didn't graduate. Then he moved on to be a car salesman with BMW, and then Maserati.

When I was in sixth grade, my mom went and got her teaching degree. Now she's still a kindergarten teacher in the same district that I grew up in. Her passion is to help kids. She saw all my friends growing up, and their backgrounds and the issues they had to overcome. She was able to help them. She loved all of them, so she's able to now start with the young kids and take them under her wing as well in that area, too. She loves doing that.

My sister and my dad, though, weren't very close. At first, my relationship with my half-sister from my dad's previous marriage wasn't very good. I didn't see her very often, but now we're pretty close. She's come to visit here a couple of times and stayed with me. She still lives in Sacramento.

When I was fifteen, in high school, I was playing tennis and swimming. The district I was in, the area that we were in as far as school, there wasn't a ton of competition for me in high school tennis or swimming. I went in freshman year at tennis and went straight into number one singles right away. I pretty much played number one singles the whole time. Then, same thing with swimming, I captained the swim team by sophomore year, then it just set up almost easy for me. We were able to build the team, though. That's what I was proud of in high school, being able to build the tennis team and the swim team up to being competitive in our league and in our section. And then, when I graduated college, I was able to come back and coach my high school tennis team, and we won the league when we did that, so that was a lot of fun. That was really cool.

I was big, big, big into, obviously, tennis, swimming, wrestling, and I did a bit of water polo as well in high school. In my junior year, I was the first person in the history of the state of California to make sections in two sports at the same time in the same season: tennis and swimming. No one had ever done that in the history of California before.

Then, in my senior year, I did it again, so I was the first person to do it twice. That was my crowning achievement in high school. That was what I thought. I went to college thinking I was a big deal because of that. Then you go into college, and you're like, "Ah, who the hell cares? Shut up." Bam, I was hit with a strong dose of reality.

Doing sports, with mock trial and everything, those were some of my favorite memories from high school. My wrestling coach, though – you think you look to a coach to be a role model, but he was one of the people that actually tried to deter me from it because we had a state-champion wrestler that was my year. We were the same weight and everything, but he was from Ukraine. It was something stupid. We were doing our athletic awards at the end of the year, and I got the award for Athlete of the Year for making the sections. The Ukrainian student had won state that year for wrestling, so the wrestling coach thought that guy should have got it. Then, when I got it, he made a big stink in front of everybody at the award ceremony, like, "Oh, that's bullshit," and I was like, "Wow, you were my coach, too." That just pushed me harder. I didn't wrestle the next year, obviously, but I focused more on the tennis and the swimming because every year, with swimming, the times get harder to qualify. They make the times harder, so then I almost didn't qualify again, and I had to keep going until I finally got it.

The wrestling coach would come up to me, and he'd trash-talk me a lot. He'd just be like, "Why aren't you wrestling anymore? You don't want to deal with the big boys anymore?"

I was like, "What do you mean? What are you talking about? I have my other sport that I'm focusing on." That was one of the things that pushed me. I wouldn't say he bullied me, but just that you will have haters. He was one of those, apparently, which was weird because I enjoyed wrestling. That taught me it doesn't really matter that other folks are going to criticize whatever you do. That was a thing: When I did it, I was like, "Oh, yeah, I'm going to be hot shit."

Then, when he said that, I was like, "Oh, okay. I guess not. I guess, no matter what you do, someone somewhere is going to find some way to try to deter you from doing whatever it is you want to do." Then I focused mainly on: They're going to say what they're going to say, and I'm going to just do my thing, and the people I want to have around me or that want to be around me, they'll be around me. The people that don't, won't, and you move on from there.

Then, moving on to college, originally, I got into University of the Pacific. I got offers from a couple of other schools, like California Lutheran University. They wanted me to play tennis and swim for them. I said, "No, I want to have a life," so I went to Pacific, and they wanted me to swim. They didn't offer me a scholarship or anything for swimming. I got an academic scholarship, but they wanted me to swim as well. Then I thought to myself, "You know what? This is going to be a tough major that I'm in. I think I'm just going to focus on this." Then I found rugby when I went to Pacific, and in my first semester, I did school and rugby. I didn't party or do anything that first bit of my freshman year. My GPA came out at a 1.9, and that was with me trying.

So, I said to myself, "You know what? Maybe physical therapy and sports medicine aren't for me. I'm not good at memorizing things like that, and I think I'm more of a people person," so then I switched majors the second semester to sports management, and then bumped my GPA up. When I finally graduated, it was about 3.2 or 3.3. Then I was partying, so I was able to enjoy myself, do rugby, and I still got good grades and was comfortable with what I was doing.

Originally, when I went into sports management, I wanted to be a sports agent. I wanted to be Scott Boras. Then, going into my senior year, I changed that. I was more upon a slacker kind of thinking. My thought right then was, "I just don't want to keep doing this school stuff," so I didn't want to go to law school. I said, "No, I'm just going to figure something else out."

I didn't want to be a sports agent, and I just said, "This is something I'm not willing to put in the work for, so it's just not worth it."

Then, in my senior year, when we were playing rugby, we were going for a national championship. We won our D-3 national championship that year, which is big. That was what I really focused on, more so than my classes. I focused on rugby those four years, which may or may not have been the smartest thing, but I loved it, and I wouldn't change it now. About January of my senior year, I was dating this girl in a sorority, and her dad was a tennis pro in Carmel, California. He worked for this company called Peter Burwash International, and I met him one day when I went out to visit them in Monterey.

We were playing tennis, and I said, "This is a cool job you have." I was just talking to him about his job, and he showed me the PBI magazine, all the places where they go, and all the places where they have different pros. I said, "Whoa, man, I wish I hadn't stopped playing tennis."

Then he said, "I saw you hitting. You'd be fine. You're not playing professionally. You're just teaching. We teach you guys stuff."

So, I thought, "Oh, really? Okay, well, I'll think about that," and I had that in the back of my mind for a second, like, "Oh, that would be really cool, but fat chance of that happening." I thought it would be cool for me, but I just thought, "I haven't played tennis in so long, I just don't know where my skills would be in being able to do it."

Then I said, "Oh, what the hell. I'll interview," and then, about two weeks before graduation, I interviewed. I had no job lined up after graduation. I was just sitting there waiting and hoping.

I interviewed to manage at Target. I was hoping to get an internship in South Africa with a rugby team out there, but then that fell through because my family member, who was going to help me, left the school that he was working at in South Africa. So that fell through, but then, after the interview with PBI, they called me back, and said, "Hey, if you work at this camp this summer, we'll see how your skills develop throughout the camp. Then you can come in, and we'll hire you."

So, I did the camp in Maine that summer, and then I came back home, coached my high school tennis team for a little bit, and then moved out to Georgia, and I became a tennis pro out here at Reynolds. I've been able to travel to the Caribbean. I've been able to travel to Austria and all that with tennis, something I never thought I'd be able to do. I never thought I was ever good enough at tennis to do anything like that.

I asked him: You didn't play on your college team. You played in high school but didn't play for four years competitively, and then you met a girl whose dad was a tennis pro, interviewed, and did a summer internship at a tennis camp in Maine coming from California? That had to be a culture shock.

Yeah, a little bit. The cool thing about that experience was the people at that camp. There were people from South Africa, New Zealand, Louisiana, California, all around, the Netherlands, everywhere. There were people from literally everywhere there, so it was cool to see the diversity. Diversity has been the main thing that shaped my life: being able to see people of different backgrounds, different places, and trying to gain an understanding of their cultures and their upbringings. I think that's definitely been helpful for me in my life.

And you've been able to look past stereotypes of skin color, hair color, tall, short, round, or skinny. You've probably been treated well by all colors and treated poorly by all colors, as we all have.

Absolutely.

How long have you been a tennis pro?

Seven years now.

Did you get placed here in Georgia from California?

Yes.

Had you ever been here before?

Nope. I came here on November 13th, 2013. I knew one person here in Atlanta because he worked at the camp that I had worked at in Maine. That night, I flew in, went with him for that day, and hung out. Then, the next morning, we met with PBI folks at the hotel lobby, and then we came out here to Reynolds and did our training for a month. I knew no one. Then, right away, when they finished up our training, I went to the Caribbean for a month because they wanted me to help out with the Christmas season, and this was right around the holidays. I was there from December 20th to mid-January. I flew back here right when we had the Snowpocalypse.

When I flew back, I came from the Caribbean in flip-flops. I've got on shorts and a polo shirt, because I always wanted to dress nice, like, "Oh, okay, I'll just wear a collared shirt." Then the plane lands, and the pilot announces, "Hey, it's nineteen degrees outside, by the way." Great. Then I got a rental car from there and drove out here, and then . . .

Started a completely new life.

Yes.

What has been a surprise to you about being a tennis pro that you didn't expect, going in?

Actually, I was worried, coming in, despite the fact that I've played tennis my whole life, that it was probably the hardest sport for me to grasp. Every other sport I did came easily. Swimming came easy; wrestling came easy; rugby came easy. It took a lot, a lot, a lot of work for me to be even presentable or any good at tennis. I think that helped me become a tennis pro more so than having a natural talent for it. You can be an amazing tennis player, all the talent in the world, but it's the fact that I didn't know what I was doing in tennis at first, and I was just trying, that I had to really focus and learn all the ins and outs of it, that makes it easier for me to teach it. If it just came naturally for me, you'd say, "Hey, James, how do I hit a forehand?"

I would answer, "I don't know. You just do it. What do you mean?"

But now, someone tells me about an issue, and I can respond, "Oh, I know. I had a problem with that. This is what helped me." I think that not having the tennis talent helped me with teaching it, and being patient with other people while teaching it. I was a swim coach during college, too. In the summers, I would coach swimming for the city of Sacramento. As far as coaching a swim team, I was able to do that. That was good, but teaching someone how to swim who doesn't know how to swim? Oh, I was stuck. I had no idea how to teach anybody how to just swim because I would just tell them, "You do it. I don't know. What do you mean, 'How do I swim?' It's just like you asked me how to walk. Just move your arms and move your legs and stay afloat."

I think it's good that things I thought were going to be disadvantages to me being a tennis professional actually ended up being advantages, just because it allowed me to have better empathy with people in teaching them.

Here you are as a tennis pro, and the reason you're a good tennis pro is that you understand it's hard for you to pick up. There's the part that people don't see, and they think, "Oh, well, he's a tennis pro. He's always been good at tennis." No, he struggled at tennis. That was his worst sport. He's a good pro because he understands the frustration of it not coming naturally.

Absolutely. My parents started me playing when I was five. If I've been playing since I was five, I should be a way better player than I am.

What were your disappointments or rejections that guided you to this point? What would people be surprised to learn that you overcame?

In my sophomore year of college, I got an injury from rugby. It was kidney trauma. I made a tackle; I was getting up from the tackle, and someone's cleat goes right in my lower back and flattens me back down to the ground. I didn't even think about it. I had bruises on my back but got up and kept playing. The next day, I'm going to the bathroom, and blood starts coming out. Me being a college sophomore, I think, immediately, STD, so I ended up going to the hospital. When I was in there, they said, "Had you come a couple of days later, you would've had renal (kidney) failure, but you have severe kidney trauma."

So, they had me on an IV all night, trying to flush it out, and then they put me on pain pills. There was a buddy of mine, at the same time, snapped his leg straight in half in a game. We were both friends. We hung out and partied together. We ended up getting into depressive states, and we both got a pill dependency for a good couple of months.

One day, I was in our apartment and, essentially, I had taken a bunch of pills, and I was throwing up in the toilet. My buddy comes into the house, comes up the stairs, and sees me. He's furious, not that I took all his stuff, but that I let it get that far. That night, he literally beat the hell out of me. The next day, I was walking to class with black eyes and still had dried blood on my mouth from it. People, a lot of the time, just assumed it was nothing, because we were always beat-up from rugby. This guy who was a campus public safety officer, he came up to me and said, "Did you have a rough practice last night?" because he always saw us coming back from practice.

I said, "Yeah," and I still had the bottle of pills in my pocket.

Then he was driving away and said, "Okay, well, take care of yourself."

I was like, "Yeah," and then, I don't know why I did it, what compelled me to do it, but I said, "No, you know what? No, we didn't have a rough practice yesterday." I took the pill bottle out of my pocket, and I gave it to him. I said, "I think I have a problem. You punish me if you need to, do whatever you need to do to me, but I just don't want this anymore," and I gave them to him.

He came up to me, takes them, and he says, "I'm not going to punish you or anything. What I am going to do is, every time I see you from now on, I'm just going to say, 'Hey, James, do you have anything for me?' That's all I'm going to say." He said, "If you do, go ahead and give it to me. If not, great."

Then he always did. Whenever he'd see me, he'd say, "Hey, James, you got anything for me?" And that's how he'd start off every conversation.

One time, I did have pills, and I was about to go take them, and he caught me halfway there. He knew. Then I was like, "Oh, you know what? Yeah, I do have something for you."

He nodded, "Okay, thanks."

I said, "Here you go," and that was it. He definitely was one of those people who taught me that I'm really lucky to have a lot of people to support me. My friend who beat me up that night was like, "Hey, get it in your head. What the hell are you doing?" Then other people that were around who cared enough to help me out without being judgmental, they were just worried about my safety. That was really cool to see, and it was humbling. It was really humbling to experience that and have people like that around me.

Moving forward throughout my life, that's helped me with always wanting to help and look out for people – see how people are doing. I've been blessed with people who have been like that for me. It would be a slap to everyone's face if I didn't want to help people. That's why I really, really love what I do now because I get the opportunity to help. I'm around kids; I'm around people of all ages. I can help them with the sport that I love and that they love too, and I can help them grow that love in it. At the same time, I want to be more than just their coach. I want to be somebody who says, "Hey, you can feel comfortable to talk to me about whatever it is." That's my big thing. I always want to be able to help folks because that's been, for me, a big defining struggle. It didn't last particularly long, but it definitely was something that resonated with me for a long time.

What is something you would pass along to the readers of this book who are looking, as a late-bloomer with a different career or a new path?

There's no timeline on success. Success isn't necessarily setting out and getting the result that you originally wanted. That doesn't always mean success. It's the things that you find along the way, different experiences that help define your success. Going into college, I never thought I was going to be a tennis pro. I thought, "If I'm not a physical therapist doctor or a sports agent lawyer, then I didn't do it," but now, I feel successful because I'm happy with what I'm doing, and I pursued what I wanted to do at the end of the day. I go to work, and I enjoy myself. I have great relationships, great people around me. That's how I define success: The different people around you, how you've impacted them, and how they've impacted you, and what you've done with it is what defines success, not always achieving necessarily that one goal that you set out to do.

If the American dream is you go out and get the nice car, the big, nice house, and the wife that's not even genetically possible, some people do that. Some people do that, and they're able to make it. They get the house; they get the car; they get the beautiful trophy wife, and they're still not happy. Would you call that successful if you're not happy? But there are people that live down the road who don't have a pot to piss in, but they're happy. I would call them more successful. They love what they have. Whatever it is, love it. Whatever you have and whoever is your family, love them. Then you're successful.

Chapter 9

John Maxwell

Let's take a break from the stories, and review a speech by John Maxwell. You'll see how the actions steps are an integral part of every story in this book.

The Mindset of a Billionaire – Learn How to Think Correctly. By John Maxwell at www.johnmaxwell.com.

You can find this speech on YouTube. It is 5:28 long and has 2.8 million views as of October 2020.

I will teach you how to think correctly. The largest gap between successful and unsuccessful people in life is the thinking gap. I'm not talking about being smart. I'm not talking about an IQ. I'm talking about **how** you think, how I think. Successful people think differently than unsuccessful people. Wise thinking leads to right living. Stupid thinking leads to wrong living. If you want to have a fulfilled life you have to fill your mind correctly. Right now, you need to focus on **today.** What I realized, and so many leaders don't understand, is that today truly matters. We overestimate what we could do tomorrow, we overexaggerate what we did yesterday, but we underestimate what we can do right now. The only time you have, the only time I have, is **now.** So, the question for all of us is what am I doing with **now?**

The great leaders, they're present in the moment, and because of that, they maximize the moment. If you are tempted to take that far-away glance, well, glance, but get right back to the present moment, because today you're preparing to make tomorrow a success.

We all want to be motivated, and yet, so many times we fail to find the secret of motivation. Let me give it to you quickly. Just do it. Motivation is not the cause of action, it's the byproduct of action. There's a lot of difference. If I think motivation is the cause of my action, then I'm going to wait to be motivated before I do something. If I realize it's the byproduct of my action that I'll start doing something, and then guess what, motivation will come up and ZAP you, and all of a sudden, you feel good and you're glad you're doing it, you're saying "Wow! This is truly wonderful!" So, let it be the byproduct to your life! Don't let it be the foundation for the actions that you take!

Nothing comes to you until you commit yourself. Nothing comes to you if you're just going to try but you're not committed. Nothing comes to you if you're just thinking about it! It's not until you take the action step. It's not until you take the direction, and do the things, will it start to flow into you!

I'm saying don't cheat yourself out of the possibility of the potential that's on the other side of commitment! Stay with it long enough to find out if there's any fruit in it. You can do goal-setting with a pencil, but you have to do goal getting with your legs. You have got to take action. And it's the action that separates us. The greatest gap in this world is the gap between knowing and doing. Knowing is goal-setting. DOING...now *that* is goal achievement.

People that are knowledgeable about habits say that it takes thirty days for a habit to become a habit. Now habits can be good, and habits can be bad. Over a period of time you can either be developing habits that are going to help you, or developing habits that are going to hurt you. People that grow develop habits that help them. The great value of a good habit is you don't have to think about it. That's why it's a habit. In other words, once you begin to practice something as good, over days and times and periods; after a while, it becomes automatic to you! It becomes who you are. In fact, I always tell people practice a good habit long enough to make it yours. Once it's yours, now it's automatic. Every day, you'll do what you should do. Often, I have the expression that everything worthwhile is uphill. That's a fact. You've never heard someone talk about accidental achievements. You've never heard of someone that got to the top of the mountain, and somebody asked them, "How did you get there?", With a confused look on their face say "I have no idea". They know how they got there. The reason they know how they got there is because they had to walk all the way up the mountain. Nobody lifted them! There were no shortcuts! There's not an elevator. There's not an escalator. It's all effort to get you to the top of the mountain.

What I want you to understand is that inspiration does a lot better when it's coupled with perspiration. There are a whole lot of people, they want to be inspired in great things, but they don't want to do the hard work to achieve those great things. It's not either/or it's both/and. So, I really trust today that you will just kind of roll up your sleeves, look at something you haven't tackled for a while, and Dive In! You'll be amazed that once, after you do the work, you'll get inspired! Don't wait to get inspired before you do the work.

There are no limits to what you can accomplish, except the limits you place on your own thinking.

It's going to be hard, but hard does not mean impossible.

Chapter 10

David

M y name is David, I'm fifty-eight, and I currently work at data analytics at a bank, with a Masters in Applied Statistics. I am responsible for fraud and anti-money laundering models detecting potential criminal activity and/or risk to the bank, whether financial or reputational. My responsibilities include validating that the models are used appropriately, such as, a card fraud model is used to detect suspicious card transactions and not check writing activities.

On the outside, I had an idyllic childhood. I had a variety of friends from many different socio-economic groups and ethnic backgrounds. I went to a private Catholic school from kindergarten through high school. I didn't have any favorite games but I loved being outside. I took oil painting lessons, and enjoyed drawing. I was an asthmatic, and lived a non-athletic life. In fifth grade, I wanted to be an architect when I grew up. My mother was a housewife, and in her later years, worked as a receptionist for a funeral home, which she absolutely enjoyed. My dad was a tile setter working for himself. We were expected to work with him on weekends, holidays, and summers, which instilled a value of honest everyday hard work.

Behind closed doors, my father was a compulsive gambler. He would lose huge sums of money at the track. We often went without even the basic necessities as children. At times when my dad's work was sparse, meals were lean, and at times, just a sandwich. Every school year, we got a new uniform and new shoes. One year, the soles of my shoes wore out and I had holes that let in rainwater. Knowing my parents did not have the money for a new pair or to fix them, I never told them, and did a patch on my own that got me through the remainder of the year. The dentist was a luxury, and for a few years I lived with a cavity that luckily did not bother me, but again, never told my parents. I did get it fixed after getting a job post high school graduation.

When I was sixteen years old, my father left us for a nineteen-year-old girl. I was suddenly the head of household. I was the proxy father to my siblings, and made sure they did their homework; completed chores at home such as putting their clothes away and keeping their room clean; made sure they were not wearing their school clothes to play in; helped them with homework; made sure they were fed when my mom was at work or away. It was a lot for a sixteen-year-old to comprehend. My guiding principles were to be honest, work hard, and get a good education.

College wasn't in the cards for me after high school. I went to a Catholic high school where they taught us college was important, and necessary to succeed and have a prosperous career. When I could not go to college, I felt that I would be a failure, and it was difficult feeling that I would ever improve my life. It was ingrained in me that I wanted to attend college. Many of my fellow classmates and friends did go to college, with some succeeding, and others not so much. That ranged from getting married and raising a family, to health issues, and for an unfortunate few, there were drug addictions. Periodically, I look back and realize that I succeeded without college. We ultimately owned and operated a successful home remodeling business. The Catholic school should have told me that was a possibility, as that would have done wonders for my self-esteem at a fragile age. To their credit, they saw more in me than I did, and encouraged me to be my best at whatever I did.

My job as head of household was to make money to keep our family fed and housed. I landed a job with a commercial construction company, which eventually led to a successful eleven-year career with another company. I worked for a hotel furniture installation company specializing in luxury hotels, such as Ritz Carlton, Sheraton, and Hilton. I was a project manager, responsible for a crew to receive and set up furniture in the guest rooms and public areas. I scheduled the deliveries, and oversaw the contractor installing carpet, wallpaper, and draperies, while working with the designers and construction company building the hotel. This was another company, and not the remodeling business I built.

Throughout my career, I kept thinking about college. In the early years of the twenty-first century we had a thriving construction business, remaining booked upwards of eighteen months in advance. That is, until the technology bubble in the stock market burst. During that time, several large jobs were put on hold by the customers, providing my partner Norman and myself and opportunity to take a breath and decide what the future would hold, regarding the business and our careers. Norman knew I wanted to go to college, so at his suggestion, I took the plunge. We both knew we were getting older and slower with our work. We also were concerned that the highly physical work we did would eventually take its toll on our bodies and health. This was the catalyst for college, and the beginning of a huge career change.

The first obstacle was the entrance exams. I failed the math test. After over twenty years of being out of school, I couldn't remember anything from my high school math classes. My first two semesters included remedial math.

Another challenge was knowing that life would be put on hold, for classes and homework. I had a partner, so the typical family lifestyle was not an issue. I did not go to many parties or dinners with neighbors or friends in lieu of homework and studying. We took fewer vacations, and coordinated time off between semester breaks, as I went to the mini May semesters and summer school, in addition to the fall and spring sessions. Any time away from school was split between resting and smaller business jobs as we were still operating the remodeling business, but on a much smaller scale such as kitchen backsplash, tile, and bathroom or kitchen remodels only. We were financially sound, so going to school was not a financial burden.

Additionally, I didn't know what tract to pursue. Which would be the quickest and most advantageous for a person my age? I chose probability and statistics, as my original plan was to be an Actuary. I chose this as I could move quickly into the profession, working most likely in the insurance industry, and the salary was at the top for mathematical professions. I did not pass the first test, and at that time, began working in the banking industry in the areas of financial loss risk prevention.

I dressed business casual for school, while there were students who came in with sweat pants, lounging clothes, and house slippers and frazzled hair. I was also in a few classes where the younger generation sat in the back and talked throughout the class, disrupting the teacher. A few times, I stood up and told them to either shut up or get out, as the teacher had little control over their class. While many were serious students, there was that subset that was forced to go to college by their parents and did not take it seriously.

I feel that non-traditional students go because they want to, and are ready for the challenges, given that many have families, careers, and obligations; whether caring for an elderly parent, maintaining a house, grocery shopping, and the like. The younger students who went above and beyond were those who were smarter, and in a few instances, I know, became very successful. For a non-traditional student; while there were a few who did what was necessary, the majority were there to better themselves or became increasingly marketable and employable. Being a non-traditional student, I was already a responsible adult, so putting school first and being successful was just natural.

I was always tempted and often did too much, as I wanted to prove to myself that I was smart and capable, while wanting to get that A. Yes, it was a problem as I would become fixated, and ended up making myself sick to my stomach, and nervous that all the time and effort would end up getting a B or C grade. I would reach a point where the project was not fun and a learning opportunity, but became this deliverable that I just needed to complete with the work being of lesser quality than if I had just stopped when the project requirements were fulfilled.

Looking back, I was an adult at sixteen, and helped my mom raise two siblings. While I did not have the opportunity to be a teenager, I would not trade it, as it made me who I am today. I have a wonderful life, am financially sound, and have a bright future.

What I want to pass along to your readers is that you are never too old to go to school, as I started college at forty-one (taking remedial math), earning a bachelor's degree and a master's degree of applied statistics. Never be afraid to take chances. While sometimes you may fail in the short term, in the long run you will win, and become the owner of your life.

Chapter 11

Shon

My name is Shontorial. Friends and family call me Shon for short. I am from a small town called Sparta, Georgia, in Hancock County. It is one of the poorest towns in Georgia. It used to be a thriving town a long time ago, but then, when the politics changed, everything started moving out of Sparta. I grew up with very humble beginnings. My dad was not in the home with me, but he was present in my life. Growing up without a father living in the home put a void in my heart. That was a part of me that was missing. I grew up in a home with another family, so we lived in a blended family which consisted of my uncles and my grandmother.

Growing up in a small town, I felt like I didn't have the right last name. By this I mean, in a small town your status is sometimes determined by your last name, who you know, what family you belong to, and if your family is prominent in the community or not. This often determines how you are treated in school, how you are categorized or stereotyped, whether you will get the bank loan, or job you applied for, in that particular community. Because my family's last name was not prominent in the community, I didn't think that I was good enough. To add to the misconception of feeling that I was not good enough, my voice was very soft, and I was quiet, and I felt overlooked when I was in school and not so popular. Despite this, I always had big dreams and aspirations. Growing up, I loved to draw, that was my passion. I loved to write, and I loved to draw, as a child. That was the creative and expressive part of me.

All throughout school, I was an obedient student, with good grades. By the time I got into the eleventh grade, peer pressure set in, and I wanted to be like everybody else. I met this guy who, surprisingly, is now my husband, and he wasn't the likely one that I should have been dating at the time. We got married when I was twenty-four years old. We both knew that we never wanted to bring our children up in a broken home, so we decided the best decision was for us to marry, and make a life together. Although we were both young, throughout the years, we learned how to grow together and complement each other. Everything that we have built, we have built together, and we have worked hard to accomplish milestones in our lives. Often, it felt like we were just parents, versus husband and wife, because we both started so young.

My story is, I got pregnant and had a child at seventeen. As a teenage mother, it was embarrassing. I felt ashamed, and I felt like I had disappointed myself, my parents, and others who did not expect this from me. One thing is for sure, I had to grow up and mature a lot faster than I would have liked to. I missed out on the opportunity to simply live as a normal teenager in my senior year of high school, and experience the traditional college life. If I wanted to go out to the movies or have a good time with my friends, I had to think about my first priority, which was my daughter, and making sure I had child care. These are not activities that a normal teenager would do. The positive aspect is, I had a supportive mother, family, and father of my child. Despite being a teenage mom, I still graduated high school on time. The downside is, I didn't go to the college that I desired, because I had to stay behind and take care of my daughter. Overall, the biggest challenge for me as a teenage mother was that I had to put all my dreams and aspirations on hold. With that being said, I did attend a community college. The beautiful irony of this story is, my daughter is now thriving today and doing very well, and she's in college herself. She had the experience of watching me work hard, and get through college while maintaining full time jobs. While attending college to complete my associate's degree, I had the opportunity to work at both community banks in my home town, so it was almost like there was this part of my life where I felt ashamed because I was a teenage mom and that I did not fit in because I didn't have the right last name (prominent last name in the community). But, in essence, it was almost like God always favored my life, so he allowed me to be able to come in contact with people that had favor for me.

Anyway, after struggling with being a full-time mother and working, I finally graduated from a community college called Georgia Military College. Then I went to University of Phoenix, where I got my bachelor's degree in psychology. My mindset was, I never wanted to be held up just because I was a teenage mother. I wasn't going to fall into that stereotype, so I had to work hard. I worked my butt off to get where I am today. It was not easy. I had a young daughter; I was going to college every day; plus, I was working. By the time I finished my bachelor's degree, I decided I wanted to get my master's degree. I knew that I loved helping people because of working in customer service, but it was a deeper desire to help people, so I decided to go into counseling. At first, I went to University of Phoenix to get my master's in psychology, but it just wasn't the best fit for me. I could not keep up with it. It was just like something was telling me, "There's something more."

I didn't listen; I just was ambitious. Eventually, I ended up flunking out. But there is a beautiful story behind it. There was something that was ringing in my head saying Liberty University, so I Googled Liberty University, and that's where I fell in love with professional counseling. I applied and got enrolled at Liberty University to take up a master's degree of arts in professional counseling. In the midst of all of this, while I'm enjoying Liberty – I loved the school very much – I was traveling back and forth to Virginia to do my counseling intensives. In the process of just growing and developing into myself, my husband and I changed churches. There was this pastor, and his name was Alexander. He was very influential in our lives. He spoke into our lives, and said, "Well, you can do this," and, "You can do that. You're going to be great." I was like, "Me?" I never thought of it that way. He played a major part in our lives, and we were just moving into this church. He also encouraged my school endeavors, and would cheer me on to finish. It was three, four, five long years because, guess what? In between that time, life started happening, and I never finished my master's degree. Not to mention I had just gotten pregnant with my second child, so there was a lot going on in that time. I had just taken the trip of a lifetime to Israel to study abroad. A year after I came back, I found out that I was pregnant, so there's a big twelve-year age gap in between my children.

After a year or two of going to this church, attending Liberty for my master's degree and having my second child, my pastor died all of a sudden. That really took a toll on us. We didn't know how to handle grief, being a young married couple. Not to mention I had just had my second child, so there was a lot going on physically, mentally and emotionally, that helped to delay my progress of finishing my master's degree. Presently, I am one internship away from my master's, but I believe it is destiny. I believe it was part of my life path.

After I had my second child, I began to experience postpartum depression and maternal depression. Nobody could really understand how I was feeling; nobody really understood what I was going through. I breastfed my child exclusively, but I also went back to work at the Head Start Program, and so that was another hard thing for me to do because nobody understood the culture of nurturing your children that way. It was like I had a pump attached to me, and then I felt ashamed at work. I could just hear and see people talking about me because that's the way that I chose to care for and nurture my child.

I started experiencing depression even though I was getting my master's degree in professional counseling. I was trying to fix myself, and I couldn't because I didn't necessarily understand why I was feeling the way that I was feeling, even though I learned everything in the textbooks.

Fast forward: A year after having my second child and losing my pastor, I lost my sister. That was the dagger that was stabbed into my heart, on top of not properly dealing with the grief, loss and life adjustments before this event. It just felt like somebody took a dagger and just ripped my heart out, because that was something that I did not expect, and it was the way that she died. I will never forget it. I just had a feeling that something wasn't right. My husband called me at work, and he said, "Where are you?"

I said, "I'm at work."

He was crying, and he said, "I'm on my way to work, but I'm about to turn around. Doctor P. (my boss at the time), is on her way to come and get you and take you home."

I said "What? What's happening? What's going on?"

He said, "Well, I don't feel right with anybody else telling you, but, Shon, someone broke into your sister's home and murdered her."

I couldn't believe it. The initial shock was, "No, let's get the facts first. That's not true. Let's just see what's going on." I was literally about to go into a panic attack. The people on my job around me, they tried to comfort me and calm me down. It was a day that I will never forget because I remember someone coming into the office, locking the door, and not letting anybody else come in because they didn't want anybody bombarding me.

It was the longest day of my life. We had to go to the police department, didn't really know much information, didn't know what was what. All we knew was that they were saying that my sister was murdered, and it was on Facebook before we even knew it. My friends knew before I even knew it, and so they were calling me to see if I knew what was going on. I had no clue; I had no idea.

Fast forward: My sister left a daughter behind. I had to help my mom plan her funeral. My oldest sister was the one who was actually strong enough to talk with the District Attorney to make sure that my sister's killer was brought to justice. We had to go through all of that: the rumors, the lies, just the negative thinking, the wondering, "Who is it?" It was just a time in my life that was a bad dream that I just wanted to wake up from at any time. That put fear and anxiety in me, and people didn't really understand the grief I was going through, so I experienced major depression.

My son was going on two at the time, so it may be about five years ago. That's a year of my life that I just want to forget.

It was probably about a year before we ever went to court – maybe two. We just had to sit there and listen to everything, even down to seeing the pictures of her body when she was murdered.

Just seeing that was traumatic – how they tied her up. We saw that in court. Not only was she killed, but there was another guy involved who was just in the wrong place at the wrong time, and they shot him too. Her murder was the result of a home invasion.

So, you have two families here: our family, and then the other family was a white family. Through that experience, we came together. We shared the one thing in common: We wanted justice for our loved ones. It was their brother and our sister. We had to sit there and come face to face with these people who possibly murdered my sister. It was three people that they caught at the time, and they're thinking that it could be more. They don't know. One guy got off, and there was a girl involved who they believe had it all set up and who knew my sister, but she just didn't know it was going to go that far. She's in prison with no possible parole. She's in jail for life. The one guy got off. The other guy is in prison, too, without parole.

Yeah, so how DO you recover from that? Well, perseverance. It was my faith – my faith in God. That's when I had to trust him the most, when I was the most fearful, when I felt the most anxious, when I felt like I couldn't leave my house without somebody watching me, or I couldn't leave my house without stereotyping people. "Did you do it? Did he do it?" I needed help, and I knew it because I could not explain my emotions. I remember, one day, driving into work, and it was raining. I had to call in to work because I was just straight-out bawling in the parking lot. I called my supervisor, and she said, "Shon, just go home," so I went home.

Next thing I know, my boss came to comfort me and to see about me. It's one thing when people come to comfort you, but if you've never gone through it, or if you've never experienced it, then you don't really understand the actual emotions that a person is feeling and how it really does traumatize you. You don't ever expect to hear that your loved one was killed or murdered. That's the harshest thing that you could ever hear. My husband, he was always used to the little, beautiful, sweet-wife me, but then, here he is having to deal with this grieving wife who's going through anxiety. He didn't understand what was going on.

Then I had a son and a daughter to take care of. Everybody was noticing that, okay, something is not right with Mom. I would forget things. People could take advantage of me on my job, saying that they gave me something when they didn't, but I didn't know because I couldn't remember. A lot of those days, I don't even remember how I got from Point A to Point B. That's just how depressed I was. It literally felt like a fog, like I was walking through a haze.

I remember coming to the conclusion that I needed help. That moment was the day when I fell into the counselor's office, and I was too proud to cry because I was embarrassed that, as a professional counseling student, I myself had to go through therapy and counseling. I'm used to comforting other people. When people ask me, "How are you doing?" my response is "Oh, I'm doing fine. How about you?" I'll always change the subject because I was feeling "Okay, you don't really understand anyway." Everybody tells you, "Just pray about it."

You want to tell the story, but you know they are not going to understand. I know Jesus fixes everything. He does, but, in essence, sometimes you have to go to the people that he gives a calling to – to help you. My dad couldn't understand. He's a pastor, and I would call him some days. My grandmother, she didn't understand. She told me I just had to get over it, and so did my husband. They just didn't really understand, truly, the pain that I was feeling on the inside. I was so broken on the inside. My heart was broken; it was in pieces.

It took me a full year to go through therapy and feel better. I would go weekly for an hour because I needed that. My therapist gave me the tools that I needed to overcome depression and to be successful with getting to a point of healing. I really thought that I was fully healed, but I wasn't. I had learned to cope with what had happened.

My counselor, he was great. He knew that I was a professional counseling student, so he would counsel me, but he would also give me tools that I needed to be successful in my helping people. He was like, "Whatever you need, just let me know." He was so proud of the progress that I was making, because I was just determined. I remember, one day, telling him that I just couldn't remember things. He said, "Okay, you, have a seat." Then he said, "What are you not telling me?" It was like he was looking into my soul. He called my bluff.

He started asking me a series of questions. Then he said, "Okay, it sounds like you have major depression. Would you be willing to see a psychologist for a diagnosis, and to take medication?"

I told him that I really would rather work through it on my own without medicine, and I did. He equipped me with the tools that I needed, whether it was waking up earlier in the morning, having prayer and meditation, and reading scripture. He also taught me to be aware of my feelings, and even where I carried the tension. He taught me muscle-relaxation techniques and various things of that nature. I made progress, and one day, he said, "Okay, I'm going to have to kick you out soon."

Looking back, what I should have recognized was that it was not so much the fact that she died, it was more of how she died that really traumatized me, that really had an impact on my life, that really caused all of the anxiety and trauma, because that's not natural. That's not normal. Even though death has a way of taking its toll on you no matter how they die, a murder is not normal. We live in a safe bubble, so we think, and then that happens. That will shake your world.

What I would like to pass along to the readers of this book is: No matter where you are in life, you will have challenges, but if you persevere, if you just stick with it, or if you will reach out for help, you can make it. Do not give up; don't throw in the towel. Just keep pressing your way through. It might be hard, but you'll get through.

I asked Shon where she found the mental perseverance. She responded: Wow. It was tough. Some days, I felt like I was going to lose my mind, but where I found the mental perseverance was through prayer and meditation. Those were the tools and the key to help me in getting therapy because he helped me to understand that my feelings were normal.

Jesus was treated unfairly and convicted falsely. Here's your sister, who was treated unfairly and falsely, and so you could find comfort in a similar situation – that somebody persevered through that, even knowing it was going to happen that way. It's funny that you should say that and bring up that analogy. I never will forget this, and this is a story that I tell often. I remember I was in the shower, and I was praying to God, "Just take the pain away." I was asking him to take the pain away, and I was asking him why. "Why did you allow this to happen?" He reminded me that I had to deal with it, that I had to go through the pain, but he also reminded me if he allowed his son that he loved to die at the hands of man, what more? Then I would think about my sister. It was a soft correction for me to keep going in life, that I could get through this, but I feel like, when I look back on my life, he was telling me to endure the pain so that I can help someone else.

Presently, despite my journey of humble beginnings, setbacks and delays, I am now a Certified Life Purpose Coach, Speaker, Author and Facilitator. I believe that my life path, the journey that I have had to endure has brought me into my purpose. I empower women to move forward in life through the discovery of her purpose. We work through the process of limiting beliefs, their perceived roles, and lay the foundation for mapping a vision and setting goals. Through my life experiences I now help others find their voice, find their path to living out their dreams, and seeing possibilities where there seems to be limitations.

Chapter 12

Samantha

My name is Sam, and I'm a thirty-three-year-old full-time mother of three, part-time office assistant, and part-time freelance audio/video transcriber and editor. I completed the college-preparatory program in high school, fully intending to pursue further – if not lifelong – education. Although I was accepted into traditional college, I did not qualify for enough financial aid to pay for it because due to physical limitations, I spent my last three years of high school in a distance-learning program. At the time, this disqualified me from many types of scholarships and financial aid. I had no idea until it was too late, that opting out of campus-based high school and into a correspondence program (there weren't entirely web-based options then) meant that my diploma would not be taken seriously when it came time to pay for a degree. I was still determined to pursue whatever education I could afford, so I paid out of pocket to earn a two-year certificate in secretarial studies through Penn Foster.

I was a premature baby weighing in at less than five pounds, and could not breathe independently at birth. Doctors warned my parents not to get too attached to me. Brain damage, caused by oxygen deprivation and strokes, resulted in mild cerebral palsy, but it was a few years before a physician at a Shriners Hospital for Children explained my diagnosis to my bewildered parents. Thanks to the Shriners, I had access to appropriate medical attention. I was provided with custom plastic leg braces and years of physical therapy that my parents couldn't otherwise afford. The braces were effective but difficult to hide, making them uncomfortable, ugly, bully magnets. Although I had good friends in public school, I had just as many bullies in any given school year, and a trip down the hall or by bus usually included my being deliberately knocked down and called "Gimp" or "Cripple."

I was frequently excused from class, where I was the most handicapped student, for group physical therapy sessions, where I was the least handicapped student. I remember one girl in particular who was a few years older than me, and totally dependent on special crutches. She may be the most upbeat person I've ever met, and that really affected me. It was painful to watch her struggle to complete simple tasks while I practiced walking up and down a flight of stairs, but she was undeterred and apparently impossible to discourage. I couldn't whine, complain, or fail to appreciate whatever incremental progress I was making in the presence of those other irrepressible kids who were physically worse off than I was. Since none of us had the option to be athletic, we were all generally bookish and introspective. Those kids – not to mention the wonderful physical therapist – gave me a strong appreciation for life's small favors and minor victories.

I have much to thank my parents for, too. Despite the grim early warnings from doctors not to "expect much" from me, Mom and Dad always treated me normally, and never made me feel like a sideshow or like a highly fragile item in need of constant protection. They loved, accepted, and encouraged me, which made home feel like both a retreat from the chaos, and a launchpad for adventure. The daily bullying at school was a problem and still is for many kids today, but it's far easier to cope with when you have a healthy support system because you tend to value your family's opinion over the insults hurled at you like dodgeballs on the playground. Bullying is no joke, and we certainly should be working as a society to eliminate it, but being on the receiving end of that abuse taught me compassion and empathy faster than anything else could have.

I'm ashamed of it now, but that compassion and empathy didn't extend to my sister. She is about five years younger than me, and, despite my mistreatment at school, I bullied her at home and felt like I was king of my particular hill. Maybe it was some kind of redirected hostility, but that doesn't excuse my behavior. I marginalized her and lied about her to our parents, generally making her miserable. Somewhere around the age of thirteen, I finally admitted how hypocritical I was, and started to cultivate a friendship with her. I'm lucky she forgave me. She's an intelligent, funny, fierce spitfire of a woman that anyone could learn a lot from, and I have. I shy away from confrontation, even when I shouldn't. She doesn't have the same reservations, and it serves her well.

For most of their married life, before they divorced when I was in my twenties, my parents had a functional relationship, and I always thought of them as a team. I wanted that kind of commitment, and longed to be married and have children of my own. When I was fifteen, I met a boy and promptly fell in love – or thought I did. In hindsight, I'm not sure, but I was stubbornly committed to him. We dated for a few years and married almost as soon as I turned eighteen. My family, I later discovered, staunchly thought he was wrong for me but didn't want to alienate me by letting on. They were right, of course. If I had known about their disapproval, I would have resented them and married him anyway. I was a deliriously happy wife for a few surreal months, and then my husband started treating me differently. He was distant, moody, unpredictable, and cold, sometimes not speaking to me for whole days. I was devastated and embarrassed, so I didn't tell anyone, and maintained a general show of happiness. Most of the time, he treated me like an inconvenient but necessary roommate.

We went through a tumultuous period where my husband and I had a couple of long separations, which forced me to move, change jobs, and question nearly all of my choices. After a particularly devastating nine-month separation, he insisted he wanted to get back together, which I had heard before, so I was skeptical. As a gesture of sincerity, he suggested we buy our first house. Over several months, we dated again, purchased a home, and started over, but, shortly after that, he seemed distracted and unhappy again. I obsessed over what I was doing wrong, where I was failing as a wife and friend. On bad days, which eventually outnumbered the good ones, I wasn't very kind to him either. Then, like many people around 2009, we could no longer afford our mortgage, and we faced possible foreclosure. One day, he turned to me and said, "I don't think this is going to work out; I think you need to move."

I expected to be despondent, but I was flooded with relief. It was over; I knew where I stood. It was a clean break, and I could just begin again – whatever that meant. My parents had recently divorced at the time – another long story – and my mom invited me to live with her in central Kentucky, where I'd only visited before. In a week, I had to quit a job I loved, pack up whatever I could take, load it in a friend's trailer, and head hours south where I knew no one but Mom, and had no job lined up. It would have been scary, but years of ambiguity in my marriage had created a gathering cloud over me, and moving somewhere new to start again seemed to scatter those shadows. Mom and I are good friends as adults, so there was one stable relationship I could count on, and we enjoyed being roommates. Neither of us had ever expected to be divorced, and we supported each other through our uncertain times when we both had to redefine ourselves abruptly with no idea where to begin.

My parents worked full-time jobs when I was growing up, and my mom took care of us and the house when she wasn't at work. Mom grew up on a farm until she was seventeen, where they kept pigs, horses, goats, chickens, etc. After high school graduation, she was recruited to work for an insurance company, then later became retail management. Dad was more of a city boy whose family had moved around a lot throughout his childhood. He chose to drop out of high school, earn his GED, and make a career of alternately building, repairing, and selling cars. He worked relatively long hours, and took care of the house and car maintenance when he was home. Neither of them attended college, but they are two of the smartest people I know, and I still consult them whenever I need advice.

My family is loving, but not perfect, and I learned by osmosis that if you were sitting, you were probably wasting time. Hard work is generally underrated, but what I learned smacks of workaholism, and I am still trying to shake that off and allow myself downtime. However, my work ethic has served me well in my career – mostly retail. You can teach an employee many skills, but dependability, resourcefulness, and a sense of pride in a job well done are usually a lost cause if not learned in childhood. My parents were both in sales, and I joke that I've been doing inventory since I was seven, when Mom sometimes took me to work with her. I have a natural aptitude for working on a salesfloor, so that's what I did. I didn't want to make a career out of it, but I thought it was my only marketable skill.

Naturally, when I moved in with my mom in central Kentucky, I worked in retail. Except for a short stint at a bank call center – where I discovered the soul-sucking qualities of a monochrome cubicle – retail was my entire resume. I had tried before to leverage my secretarial studies certificate and my other skills (such as writing, editing, proofreading, and computer proficiency) to land a job in an office, but without prior experience, they wouldn't hire me. Many times, I asked myself, "How does one get previous experience, then?" But my question ultimately drifted into the ether of the Wal-Mart checkout line, where I couldn't have heard the answer anyway over the beeping of my register. I was working that checkout line when I met Jacob, my then coworker and present husband. While I was checking him out, he was checking me out, you might say.

Jacob was fighting an uphill battle when he determined to get to know me. I had sworn off dating or ever marrying again, and told God – my only constant through every struggle – that I wanted to be devoted to him and his plan for me, even if it meant I spent the rest of my life single and childless. I asked God to keep me in the center of his will, even if I was dense, and he had to bypass me to do it. That had become my daily prayer after I had seen the results of my wayward choices, and read *Anonymous*, by Alicia Britt Chole. Jacob consistently and patiently invited me to sit with him and his friends at lunch, which I repeatedly declined, secretly terrified by my own attraction to him.

One fateful day, Jake recommended my next read: *The Shack*, by William P. Young. I'm a sucker for a book, and took the bait. We read the novel simultaneously, bonded over cerebral conversations about spiritual questions, and I found myself in love. I thought I was crazy and couldn't trust my feelings. I was sure Jake only thought of me as a friend, so I was overcome with conflicting emotions when he unexpectedly asked me out for coffee. It was truly the last thing I thought he would say.

I knew I had chosen wisely when Jake walked me to the front door after our first date and prayed with me instead of trying to steal a kiss. Our romance was a whirlwind, but we committed to keeping Jesus at the center of our relationship, and we were married six months after our first date. Nearly a decade later, we have three children aged seven and under, and we tease each other about still being in the honeymoon phase, although that honeymoon has included rough days.

When we found out we were expecting our first child seven years ago, I knew I wanted to try staying home with the baby. I didn't want to have to entrust my son to others while I was at work. I had also developed arthritis in my left foot, which was especially problematic when coupled with fifty added pregnancy pounds. On paper, there was no way we could make ends meet financially on one income, but Jacob encouraged me to try it anyway. Honestly, my retail paychecks would have been swallowed up by the high cost of daycare. I left Wal-Mart to became a full-time mother.

I immediately felt guilty for not being a financial contributor or working outside the home. For a while, I frantically cleaned the entire house every day and cooked all the meals, in an effort to "make up" for the fact that I didn't have a traditional job. I already carried shame because I need help with physical tasks more often than the average person, I don't drive, and my medical needs are expensive. I suddenly felt like a deadbeat mooching off my husband. Like June Cleaver, I thought everything had to be just so, and I had to look beautiful when Jacob got home, or I had failed as a wife. He thought this was a ridiculous notion, but it took me years to get over.

Staying home with my children has taught me planning, time management, strategy, self-motivation, conflict resolution, budgeting, resourcefulness, and patience in a sink-or-swim format. I no longer think of my home-based time as a gaping hole in my employment history because I have gained innumerable work/life skills that I wouldn't have otherwise learned. I discovered couponing and other cash-conserving tricks, actually saving us more money than I used to earn. I put my listening, editing, and computer skills to work by becoming a freelance audio/video transcriber, which is an education in itself. You never know who you'll be listening to or what they'll be talking about – it's often fascinating and eye-opening. I started reviewing books professionally, which I love.

One day, after reading my review of his book, a Pennsylvania-based author contacted me and asked me to edit his second book before its publication. I was thrilled and honored – remember, I don't yet have any framed degrees on my wall. I have professionally edited two books so far, and hope to edit more. On that note, I have also taken advantage of many web-based free and low-cost classes to hone my editing skills or to learn about anything that interests me, such as history, biblical subjects, etc. I think we turn up our noses at the idea of self-education or dismiss the self-educated person, to our own detriment. After all, how many inspiring historical figures were "uneducated" or self-educated?

My husband is in the throes of earning his bachelor's degree in Addictions Counseling, in part because I stayed home and pinched pennies. He has offered to return the favor when he's finished, although I have no idea what my college major would be.

I'll probably do it anyway, because if life has taught me anything it's that being unsure shouldn't slow you down – it's the starting that matters. God told Abram to leave everything he knew, and "go to the place I will show you." He got up and went without a destination, and I think God honors that if your focus is on him. Waiting for all the answers first just means you will never arrive, and even detours are rarely a waste of time in the end. Looking back, I wish I had recognized that sooner. It would have precluded so much hesitation on my part to take risks. Mistakes are a part of life, and they can teach you as much – if not more – than "success" can. In fact, I think our mistakes are a universal equalizer that would give us all common ground on which to relate to each other, if we would just be honest about them.

What I want to pass along to your readers is that you can't expect perfection from yourself, or any other person. Comparing yourself to another, or even to a younger you, is always comparing apples to oranges. Be careful not to idolize or dismiss yourself or anybody else. You are on your own path, and you will only happen once. God sees you through your struggles so that you can see others through theirs. Use your mistakes and your pain to cultivate empathy for others, and make it a point to imagine life in their shoes. Then, ask yourself how you are uniquely equipped to help. Compassion is a skill you don't need a professor for, and a life of trying to help is a career that's always worthwhile.

YouTube Search:

How to Shift Your Mindset | Mary Morrissey

7:29 minutes of pure gold.

Chapter 13

Christine

My name is Christine, I am a massage therapist and I'm somewhere around Doug's age.

I grew up in the suburbs of New York. I was born in the city, but I moved at eight years old to the suburbs with my family. I'm the oldest of three kids; I have two younger brothers. My mom and dad divorced when I was nineteen or twenty.

My baby brother has managed Home Depots and Lowe's and Advanced Auto places. He's jumped around, but he has hooked up with somebody who has an electrician company, and he is hopefully going to take over that company. He has a wife and two girls. My other brother has removed himself from the family. He lives in New York. To the best of my knowledge, he's a maintenance person at the high school we went to, and over the last several years, has made a couple of trips to Thailand to do a complete sex change. I guess now technically he's my sister. I don't like to say it like that, but...

When was the last time you talked to him?

Oh, my goodness. My daughter was born in '93, so probably '91. We emailed each other when I was trying to get him to not go to Thailand to – what I consider – mutilate his body, but he started getting nasty and just stopped emailing with me. I haven't really talked to him since.

What kind of work did your mom and dad do?

My mom did a lot of things. Mostly, when we were small, she worked in the schools we attended, probably to keep an eye on us. We hated that. She ended up retiring from Kraft Food. My dad retired from the New York Telephone Company, where he worked for as long as I ever remember.

After high school, I did anything and everything. I graduated late because I didn't have enough credits, so I had to go to summer school to graduate from high school. I worked in a lot of restaurants. I worked in a lot of retail stores. I ended up moving in with a boyfriend for about four years. We got engaged. We got unengaged. I moved out, and a year later, started dating my soon-to-be first husband. I had dated him in high school. We got back together and ended up getting married.

Did you ever go to college?

Never.

I asked: Was your dad encouraging about that?

Christine: No. No, my mother said we made too much money to get financial help and too little money to send me to college, and my dad just cut to the chase and said that I was not college material.

With a look of horror of my face I asked: Your dad said to you, "You are not college material"?

Christine: That's right.

Me: How did that make you feel?

He was telling the truth. I was only asking to go to college because everybody else was.

Rather than go to college, what did you do?

Again, I worked in restaurants, and I worked in gyms. I had a cleaning service in New York. I hadn't had any children yet. When I moved here in '92 from New York, I lived in Kennesaw. I didn't think anything about having a cleaning service there because I got a job at the leasing office at the apartment complex we moved into, and I was happy there. I had my daughter, and then, a year later, we moved to the lake area. I thought maybe I would consider doing my cleaning service, but people were not willing to pay what I was used to making, so I couldn't think about that. I babysat children in my home so I could keep my daughter home with me.

Three and a half years after I had my daughter, I had my son, and he was still in a car seat when I visited my aunt, who was fifty at the time, in Wilmington, North Carolina. She had just graduated from massage school. When the kids went to sleep, she asked me if I wanted a massage, and I got a massage from her. She told me what she went through to go to school to do it, how flexible I could have my schedule, and how much money I could make. I thought it sounded very doable, so I came back to Georgia, looked into it, got the pricing, got pretty excited about it, and presented it to my husband. He didn't think we could afford for me to go to massage school, but I decided that I needed to regardless of what his thoughts were. I thought we would just figure it out financially, and I needed to go forward with it. It was the best decision.

Tell me about your trip in the car, looking out the window.

We had it all planned that I was going to start in February of the following year. It was Thanksgiving, and we were having dinner with my husband's relatives up in Marietta. When we were driving home on I-20, it was at night, so I was looking out the window and watching all the things that you see when you're driving down the road. That's when my husband announced that it was not a good idea for me to go to school because we couldn't afford it. It was a turning point for me because, as I was looking out the window, I described being able to see everything on the other side of the window. Then, all of a sudden, because it was dark outside, I could see my own reflection instead of what was on the other side of the window. I saw my face, and it just came to me to say, "No, I'm going. I need to go." That was me putting my foot down, or using my voice. Like I said, it was really my best decision.

It was a turning point in our relationship as well because, come to find out, I needed to do something like that. I needed to feel more empowered because he really had been doing things just how he wanted to do things, even though I had a lot to say about it. He basically told me that I wasn't contributing to his income or the household, even though I was staying home with my kids and keeping other people's children to supplement his income. He didn't see it as anything of value. We were probably pretty close to a divorce by then, but I just didn't realize it. Making that decision and going to school just suddenly made me feel like, "I'm going to be okay, and I don't need anybody else." It definitely was a huge, huge turning point.

Did you have doubts?

Never. Massage school was a 550-hour course. It lasted from February to the end of December, so I graduated in December of 1999, and started doing massage on my own. I rented a room from an accountant, and my husband was suddenly all on board [but] during those first six months, he [thought] my business wasn't building up fast enough. I think, within six months, he had started gambling really bad, and with about three or four clients a week, I just decided that we needed to separate. I had him served on his job site, and we were divorced by the end of 2000.

What kind of frustrations and setbacks did you have in the early years of being a massage therapist?

I really didn't have too many. My business built like wildfire. It was a great time to be a massage therapist in this area because there weren't many, and my clients loved me. They all talked about me to their friends. My clientele built up really quickly. I really didn't have many frustrations except when I met my second husband. He had a really hard time with me massaging men. He described it as he "got physically ill" knowing I was going to have a male client. I changed my policy to women only for two years.

At the time, I was working at Southern Laser Salon, and then a chiropractor asked if I would come and work in his office. Just like I do now, I rented [an upstairs] room from him, but he needed to have [a massage therapist] on premises. I told my husband, "It's been two years [that] I've been massaging only women. You need to put your big-boy panties on because I need to start massaging men also, or else I will drown in this industry." By this time, there were many more massage therapists. So that's what happened.

Did he finally put his big-girl panties on?

No. No, actually, within three years of our marrying, his father was very, very ill, and died. His mother bought a house, and we all lived in the house together. He became more of a mama's boy than ever before. It was a house divided; it was me and my kids versus him and his mother. That didn't go well, so ex-husband number two.

So now you're at a place where you get to set your own time and have a full schedule?

Oh, yeah, that's been since the beginning. I went to all my kids' ball games. I never missed a first pitch. I never missed a tipoff. I never missed the gun for track. I was always there. They traveled; I traveled. I had the luxury of being able to do that because I could set my own schedule. My clients were very understanding; they were very good to me. There were some clients [who], when they knew that we were going out of town for a track meet, they would slip me an extra $100 to go out and get something to eat. More people than I can even count have, for example, bought my daughter a prom dress. A number of generous offerings I've gotten from my clients because they have just generally taken me and my kids under their wing.

What is something people would be surprised to learn about you?

I was addicted to cocaine when I was in my early twenties, but I am no longer even a user. I guess I had that moment of clarity because, by that time, I was smoking it, and the person I was with set himself on fire. When he wouldn't put the pipe down to put himself out, I was like, "Okay, this is getting pretty serious." I started going to meetings. Of course, that's long behind me, thank God. That was way before kids.

Good for you. Congratulations on your recovery. What is something you would like the readers – who are looking at second chances, late bloomers, folks like that – what is something you would like them to know?

It's never too late. There's always somebody in a more difficult and challenging situation than you are. If you have the desire to change direction, I would strongly encourage a relationship with God, and pray about it because prayer works. Don't ever sell yourself short, and don't let anybody's reactions to you dictate how you feel about yourself.

Chapter 14

Julia "Juju" Hook

5 Reasons Women Over 50 Should Start Something Big And New
Reprinted with permission from the Author.
www.jujuhook.com

Last February, I went to Mammoth, snowboarding with some friends. (To be totally transparent, they snowboarded. I drank Pinot Noir.) In the bar, I met a couple of women who were pushing fifty, with teenaged kids. We got to talking about life, and I told them that at forty-nine, I'd packed up my successful business to become a motivational writer and coach.

One of them said, "God, I wish I was as brave as you. I've always wanted to be a girls' basketball coach. But it's too late now. It just seems stupid. How would I even begin?"

She felt what so many women who are circling 50 feel:

It's too late. That ship has sailed. If I was going to do it, I should have done it by now.

Since that time, I've spoken to hundreds of women between 45 and 60. And I've found an alarmingly common thread: almost every one of them has a dream that's never been addressed. And they've decided to *let those dreams go*, because "50" is a force field that's impossible – in their minds – to cross.

115

I've found three distinct groups of ladies my age who struggle with this the most:

The Retirement Pushers: These women have been in jobs or careers for 20 years or more, and they see retirement as the end. The Retirement Pusher feels like it's foolish to switch gears now. She *can* finish this long, grueling haul that she started decades ago, so she *must*.

The I'm-Just-a-Moms: These women have been raising kids for 15, 20, or 25 years, and they don't feel *justified* in doing anything else. The I'm-Just-a-Mom knows she's qualified for something big and new, but thinks those things are reserved for women who started earlier in life.

The Shadow Dancers: In their 20s, these women labeled their dreams as foolish, and chose related (but sensible) careers, instead. (I chose Marketing Manager over author at 20. Just in case I wasn't Hemingway....) The shadow dancer's dream has never died; but a little bit of her soul has, every day.

Here's the good news, ladies:

Whether you dream of becoming a pastry chef, learning to surf, traveling to India by yourself, tap dancing at a recital, or opening an accounting firm, now is the PERFECT time.

Here are 5 reasons women over 50 are PERFECT for big, bold, new things:

1. We're wise. It's not the same as knowledgeable. Wise means we think and act *using* knowledge. Try this: grab a woman over 50 and give her detailed instructions for a task she's never done before. After 45 seconds she'll say, "Yeah, yeah. I get it. Let me do it." And then she'll shove you aside and do it *her* way... the more efficient way.

2. We can negotiate like hell. We've been finding ways to get what we want for decades. I've negotiated with husbands, toddlers, teenagers, airline ticket agents, hair dressers who wanna do their own thing, real estate agents, human resources directors, the DMV, the woman at the nursing home who refused to give my mom her pain meds, and the guy who showed up to fix my toilet and tried to hard-sell me a $10,000 water purification system. Women our age know how to say, "No" and how to get, "Yes."

3. We're effective. We are amazingly *useful* for achieving desired results. I can cook a delicious turkey dinner while simultaneously talking my 15-year-old down from a ledge, sending a follow-up email to a client, and planning my next vacation on Travelocity at a 30% discount. We've been conditioned to conquer tasks, *while* figuring them out. If you've got a complex problem to solve, who you gonna call? A recent college grad? Or one of your girlfriends over 50?

4. We've developed a sense of humor… about ourselves. A couple of weeks ago, I thought I'd try false eyelashes. Everyone is doing it, and I figured, "What the hell? If I can expertly super-glue a shattered vase back together in the 15 minutes before my mother-in-law shows up for dinner, I can surely get these suckers attached to my eyelids." And when I looked in the mirror and saw a drag queen in Ugg boots, I laughed like hell. Every woman I know who's my age can laugh at herself. And if you're thinking that comes just as naturally for a younger woman, too, try teasing a millennial about her false eyelashes…

5. We're resilient. I sometimes hear my friends say, "I don't bounce back like I used to." This is simply untrue. I've bounced back from divorce, crushing career blows, the painful loss of family members, more financial hitches than you can shake a stick at, and a full hysterectomy. What about you? There is simply not a single demographic group in the WORLD more resilient than 50-year-old women.

If we have everything it takes to be successful at something new, why do we feel like we're unwarranted, unqualified, or silly for wanting to start something at "our age?"

Is it because we feel like time is running out? Because every article I read says that it takes seven years to be an expert at something. And ladies… we've GOT that much time. You could cruise through your late 50's, 60's and 70's — doing the very thing you've always wanted to do. I know I fully intend to.

Is it because we're tired? I want to let you in on a little secret. You're not tired. You're tired OF something. I was tired of my old business. But I'm not tired of my new one. I'm energized, challenged, and entertained. If you're tired of picking up socks off the floor, try putting on some Barry White and dancing around with a glass of wine. Too tired for that? I rest my case.

Is it because the world tells us we can't? Ridiculous. We've all been doing things we weren't supposed to do our whole lives. (Remember Macrame? Rollerblading? Microsoft DOS?) We are a LEGION of humans who have achieved things we were never meant to achieve.

I have realized that when a single, simple ingredient is added to the recipe for dreams at our age, they rise like perfect biscuits: PERMISSION.

That's right. You have to give *yourself* permission. You have to ditch the story that's holding you back, *see* what that new role looks like, slide it on like a bada** black trench coat, and wear it out into the street. You have to give yourself permission to be that woman.

You are the perfect age for this field trip, my friend, and you've got a hell of a lot more in your backpack than your sack lunch and your library book.

How many permission slips have you signed in your life? Isn't it time you signed one for yourself?

Julia "Juju" Hook (www.jujuhook.com) was a brand strategist for more than 25 years, before she gave herself permission to follow her true passion and calling, and became a writer, motivator, and coach. Her book Hot Flashes, Car Pools and Dirty Martinis *is available on Amazon.*

Chapter 15

I need your help.

A lot of people have put time, effort and money into researching, interviewing, typing and publishing this book. I have two items to ask in return.

1) I want your story.

2) I need your association, club, business or conference director that books platform speakers.

You can reach out to me at **www.MBAat58.com**.

When I told people I wanted their story, some of them looked at me, tilted their head, and said I don't have anything worth telling. Jim, in your case, you are right! The rest of the people in this book volunteered their story without hesitation. I want your story for the next volume. Somebody is going through a hard time or difficulty and would love to hear how you overcame your setback. The USA has more than 350,000,000 people and we are only five percent of the world's population. You can be an inspiration to someone in America, or some other part of the world's population of over seven billion.

Who do you know that is looking for a platform speaker? I have been a public speaker for over ten years. I have studied my craft. Associations and conferences are always looking for a keynote speaker. My speech is titled *Transforming Mindsets Through Perseverance and Popcorn*. Sarah inspired me with the perseverance portion of this presentation. She got me to begin my day drinking twelve ounces of water. I put the cup of water on my nightstand before I go to sleep. My morning routine is to wake up, put on my glasses, look at my watch or phone to check the time, and reach for the glass of water. I don't even have to open my eyes – I can find it with my hand. Drinking twelve ounces of water a day times three hundred sixty-five days in a year is an extra thirty-four gallons of water per year. Want to do your part to avoid a kidney stone? Drink more water. Want clearer skin? Drink more water. I made cups to hand out at my presentations. It is my business card. I want all of your audience members to have one.

Perseverance:

12 Ounces/Day = 34 Gallons/Yr

Read 15 Mins/Day = 27 Books/Yr

Cut 100 Calories/Day = 10 Lbs/Yr

What's Your Story?

www.MBAat58.com

Once we connect, we'll discuss what outcomes they are expecting for their audience. If I'm not the right speaker, I'm a member of a community of speakers, and will be glad to refer them to someone else. I'm the first one to admit I'm not the right speaker for every audience.

www.MBAat58.com

Chapter 16

What's next? Help a friend.

I hope you found some encouragement from those stories. Maybe one or two of those stories made you think of someone who needs to hear of their frustrations and difficulties. It may give your friend or coworker hope, that they too will get through this obstacle they are facing. This next section of the book is about taking action in your life or helping someone who needs a step up. In the words of Dr. Wes, there are about four or five significant people in everyone's life. They stand at the fork in the road that can have a dramatic impact on your destination. How do you help your favorite grocery store cashier get her GED so she can apply for a job with your company and work in bookkeeping? Maybe she'd like to go to a junior college and get an associate's degree in bookkeeping or accounting. Nobody has taken the time to reach out, buy her lunch, and give her a plan. She could be the most dependable employee at your firm. She just needs a nudge.

Maybe you have a son, daughter, brother, or sister who would like to finish their undergraduate degree. They just need to take two more classes, but that was ten years ago, and they don't even know where or how to apply. Where would their classes and credits transfer to? They have a spouse and kids now, so they can't drive to a campus. Where could they apply to finish their courses online? There are 5,500 colleges and universities in America.

Just start.

Chapter 17

Create a vision board

Wondering what is a vision board?

You could actually use an extra theory on this one. Here is your Vision Board 101 to better understand the most powerful manifestation tool you could ever use. In one sentence, a vision board is a super-simple tool that activates the law of attraction for you, bringing all the things and experiences you desire into your life.

In this article, we'll present you with multiple vision board ideas and examples to better understand this powerful manifestation tool. You can improve every area of your life with the help of a vision board.

There are multiple types of vision boards you could use for this purpose. Today, you'll discover which type you need to get exactly what you want. Lay your eyes on the vision board ideas and examples that will change your life for good.

Types of Vision Boards:

Generally speaking, there are three types of vision boards:

1. The "I Know Exactly What I Want" Vision Board

2. The "I am Not Sure What I Want, But I Want a Positive Change" Vision Board

3. The "Theme" Vision Board

https://www.amazer.me/vision-board-ideas-and-examples-to-get-you-started/

Search in Google for "Steve Harvey vision boards".

You'll find this video that is 2:57 in duration.

Look for this 4:45 interview with Oprah Winfrey.

If those two interviews don't convince you, then they are not for you.

9 steps to creating a vision board

I have copied the highlights of the 9 steps below. You can find the full article at this link.

https://smartleadershiphut.com/visualization/vision-board/

Step 1: Select a category or context for which you want to create your vision board.

Step 2: Define within the chosen category your primary goal you want to achieve next year.

Step 3: Collect a bundle of magazines with beautiful pictures.

Step 4: Select the images that represent your goals.

Step 5: Wait a few days, and then make the final selection of the images you want to use for your vision board.

Step 6: Start making your vision board by adding pictures big and small to your dream board.

Step 7: Add some motivational quotes or words that best describe your optimal feeling.

Step 8: Now you have created your vision board, it is the time that you start to manifest your vision board.

Step 9: After some time, your vision board might need an update.

Chapter 18

How to get a GED

A re you a senior leader at your organization? How would you like more loyal employees and lower turnover? At the end of this chapter, you'll read the statistics for that statement.

The GED is named for the general education development tests one is required to pass in order to earn a GED, which is a high school equivalency diploma. In other words, your GED diploma is proof that you demonstrated the same level of understanding of high school subjects as a traditional high school graduate. Originally created in the early 1940s by the American Council on Education (ACE), the GED program provided homecoming military members who had joined the armed forces before graduating from high school with a way to prove their working knowledge of subjects covered in high school, so that they could join the workforce or pursue further education after their service.

Today, the GED serves the same function for many people, regardless of military status, who did not complete high school and need to earn a GED in order to follow their chosen career path. Earning a GED vastly expands the career possibilities of a high school non-graduate, including but not limited to healthcare, community and social service, administrative positions, sales, and legal professions. Naturally, having a GED also paves the way to pursuing a college or technical education, which widens a graduate's horizons even further.

The general education development tests (GED) cover four subjects: math, language arts, social studies, and science. Each test ranges in length from seventy to one hundred fifty minutes. In Georgia, the fee is forty dollars per subject test, making the total cost for all four tests one hundred sixty dollars. You don't have to take all four tests at once, and can space them out however you choose. GED testing is currently available in forty-seven US states and territories, many of which have now adopted online testing in addition to physical test sites. The national average cost for all four tests is one hundred nineteen dollars. Bermuda is the most expensive at three hundred dollars. In Connecticut, GED testing is free.

Since 2014, many states have adopted new high school equivalency testing programs, in addition to or instead of the GED program. You may find that your state offers two or even three total testing options, such as HiSET (High School Equivalency Test), TASC (Test Assessing Secondary Completion), or NEDP (National External Diploma Program). Indiana, Iowa, Louisiana, Maine, New Hampshire, New York, Tennessee, and West Virginia no longer offer GED testing, instead opting for one or more of these programs. This can be good news for many testers, since a few minutes of research can help you choose which testing option is best for you. For example, the NEDP is said to be the best option for high-anxiety test takers.

The HiSET covers science, mathematics, social studies, reading, and writing. The cost ranges from eighteen to ninety dollars, and varies by state. The TASC includes the same subjects as the HiSET, and fees start at fifty dollars, with the cost rising depending on the state and testing site. According to AccreditedSchoolsOnline. org, the NEDP tests on "three foundational areas (communication and media literacy, applied math/numeracy and information and communication technology) and seven life skill areas (civil literacy and community participation, consumer awareness and financial literacy, cultural literacy, geography and history, health literacy, science, and 21st-century workplace)."[1] The fees related to the NEDP are normally a few hundred dollars.

To find out which high school equivalency test programs are offered in your state, as well as the eligibility requirements, test-prep information, cost breakdown, passing scores, and whether web-based testing is available, please visit GED.com, TASCTest. com, CASAS.org/NEDP, and/or HiSET.ets.org.

Are you a senior leader at your organization? Consider these numbers for your employees:

71% – an overwhelming majority – of participants are more loyal to their employer because GEDWorks is offered.

34% – One company saw as much as thirty-four percent lower turnover among GEDworks graduates.

11% – This employer sponsored program results in eleven times more participation than reimbursement models.

Do you know somebody who is down on their luck, and needs a helping hand? Suggest these GEDWorks-participating companies.

On a side note: One of the problems for homeless people getting back on their feet is that they have no address. If they've lost their state identification card, driver's license, or social security number, they don't have a return address when reaching out to the appropriate agency. Without those documents, they can't show up for their

---

1   "Find Your State's High School Equivalency Exam" https://www.accreditedschoolsonline. org/resources/high-school-equivalency-exams/

first day of work and get registered with Human Resources. It is a more common problem than most working people realize. Some churches and homeless shelters have a program to help them.

From the United States Postal Service web site:

https://faq.usps.com/s/article/Is-there-mail-service-for-the-homeless.

A homeless person may submit an application for PO Box™ service to a local Post Office™. The Postmaster may approve the application under any one of the following conditions:

The applicant is known to the window clerk or Postmaster.

An unknown applicant submits proper ID.

The applicant provides a verifiable point of contact (e.g., place of employment, shelter, charitable institution, or social services office).

Applicants who cannot meet these conditions may be eligible to receive indefinite General Delivery service, if approved by the local Postmaster. Customers should contact their local Post Office for more information.

Chapter 19

How to finish college

According to CollegeData.com2, the average total cost of tuition and fees for the 2019-2020 school year at a public university was $10,440 for in-state residential students. For out-of-state residents, the total hovered around $26,820. Costs at private schools were naturally even higher, but don't let these statistics be a stumbling block on the path toward your education. There are many ways to offset or minimize these expenses, and financial aid is available from several sources.

To find out what type(s) of Federal Student Aid are available to you, you will need to fill out the Free Application for Federal Student Aid, a process you will repeat each school year. Your completed FAFSA will be sent to the college(s) indicated in the form, and each school will use that information to determine the type and amount of financial aid you qualify for. You will then receive an award letter from each school explaining your available aid, which will help you make important decisions about how to pay for your education.

A grant, such as the Pell Grant, is student financial aid that does not have to be paid back – unless, for example, you abruptly

---

2   "How Much Does College Cost?" https://www.collegedata.com/en/pay-your-way/college-sticker-shock/how-much-does-college-cost

withdraw from school. Grants are generally limited to a certain amount for each school year, but every little bit helps.

Scholarships are merit- or lottery-based financial aid that also do not require repayment. Merit-based scholarships are often earned based on aspects such as athletic ability or submission of a high-quality essay. Lottery-based scholarships simply require a student to enter a drawing and provide proof of enrollment. These drawings often occur at regular intervals, such as monthly. Students should be aware of scholarship opportunities, their frequency, their eligibility requirements, and their deadlines, in order to maximize financial aid. Beware of scams; you should never have to pay for scholarship information. One trusted resource is the Department of Labor's scholarship finder at CareerOneStop.org.

If their college or university participates in the Federal Work-Study Program, undergraduate and graduate students who qualify based on financial need may be able to take full-time or part-time work related to their field of study, thereby earning money to help pay for college.

Federal or private student loans are financial aid funds that must be paid back, although there are rare exceptions. First-time borrowers who take out a federal student loan must complete entrance counseling related to their subsidized or unsubsidized loan. Unlike private loans, federal student loans often have lower, fixed interest rates and flexible repayment options. To find out more about this and all other types of Federal Student Aid, visit StudentAid.gov.

https://studentaid.gov/resources/prepare-for-college/checklists

College Preparation YouTube Playlist

Curious about what college is like? Take a look at the videos in our "Prepare for College" YouTube playlist. The playlist includes such topics as "What's the biggest myth about college?" and "What's the best tip about going to college?"

https://www.youtube.com/watch?v=JrXnBiWe4_M&feature=youtu.be

A personal note on completing the FAFSA form online each year: It's tedious, temperamental, and nitpicky. As I remember it, each parent and child had their own logon, password and personal identification number (PIN). Once you got it all figured it out, you were done for the year. Next year, you got out the file folder full of details and passwords, and went at it once again.

Chapter 20

How to get YOUR MBA

https://gardner-webb.edu/learn-more/mba-10-general/

This school advertises a ten-month MBA for $20,000 all online. I saw the billboard advertising it while driving home from Charleston, SC. I know nothing more about it. Investigate it yourself.

There are expensive private schools, moderately priced public schools, and lower priced on-line schools. Will you get what you pay for? Somewhat. If you have a Harvard MBA, you're going to stand out more than my MBA from Bellevue University. As you should. Are you guaranteed to make more money five years later than me? Nope.

Research your state and local universities for the master's degree of your choice. Each school can help you identify the financial student loan process. Make sure you pay attention to the requirements for the application process. Some schools will require you to achieve a certain score on your GMAT. According to Wikipedia.org: The Graduate Management Admission Test (GMAT) is a computer adaptive test (CAT) intended to assess certain analytical, writing, quantitative, verbal, and reading skills in written English for use in admission to a graduate management program, such as an MBA program. It requires knowledge of certain specific grammar, and knowledge of certain specific algebra, geometry, and arithmetic.

On the GMAT, you will actually receive five scores:

A total score, ranging from 200-800

A math sub-score, ranging from 0-60

A verbal sub-score, ranging from 0-60

A score for your AWA, ranging from 0-6

An Integrated Reasoning sub-score, ranging from 1-8

Not all schools require a GMAT to apply to their graduate level courses. Bellevue University just required me to have an undergraduate degree that could be documented with transcripts.

Medical School

Medical schools require a MCAT. The medical college admissions test is an eight-hour test that will make you want to cry. Those are not my words, but can you imagine an eight-hour test?

The MCAT is unlike any other test you have ever taken. This exam will not require you to produce facts from memory, but rather, you will be tested on your thought process. This exam will cover four timed sections including Verbal Reasoning (sixty-five multiple-choice questions), Physical Sciences (seventy-seven multiple-choice questions), Biological Sciences (seventy-seven multiple-choice questions), and a Writing Sample (two essays, thirty minutes each).

Chapter 21

Books to read if you don't want to go back to school

This book is presented with the best intentions, but I know there are some people who don't have the time or money to go back to school. Or they just need a little direction for a specific issue. Here is a list of books that have been recommended. I have read most of them, and encourage you to read them as well. If you have a short attention span like me, then I would recommend Blinkist or Audible.

What is Blinkist? The Blinkist app gives you the key ideas from a bestselling nonfiction book in just fifteen minutes. Available in bitesize text and audio, the app makes it easier than ever to find time to read.

GRIT

The Power of Passion and Perseverance
By Angela Duckworth
Website: http://angeladuckworth.com/
Blinkist:
Grit (2016) is about the elusive virtue that allows people to do what they love, find a purpose in life and, most importantly, stick

with it long enough for them to truly flourish. Find out how you can discover your grit, and use it to follow your calling in life – and to hang in there, even when the going gets tough.

Publisher Summary from Amazon.com

In this instant New York Times bestseller, pioneering psychologist Angela Duckworth shows anyone striving to succeed—be it parents, students, educators, athletes, or business people—that the secret to outstanding achievement is not talent but a special blend of passion and persistence she calls "grit."

Drawing on her own powerful story as the daughter of a scientist who frequently noted her lack of "genius," Duckworth, now a celebrated researcher and professor, describes her early eye-opening stints in teaching, business consulting, and neuroscience, which led to the hypothesis that what really drives success is not "genius" but a unique combination of passion and long-term perseverance.

In *Grit*, she takes readers into the field to visit cadets struggling through their first days at West Point, teachers working in some of the toughest schools, and young finalists in the National Spelling Bee. She also mines fascinating insights from history, and shows what can be gleaned from modern experiments in peak performance. Finally, she shares what she's learned from interviewing dozens of high achievers—from JP Morgan CEO Jamie Dimon, to *New Yorker* cartoon editor Bob Mankoff, to Seattle Seahawks Coach Pete Carroll.

Among *Grit*'s most valuable insights:

Why any effort you make ultimately counts twice toward your goal. How grit can be learned, regardless of I.Q. or circumstances. How lifelong interest is triggered.

How much of optimal practice is suffering and how much ecstasy. Which is better for your child—a warm embrace or high standards. The magic of the Hard Thing Rule. Winningly personal, insightful, and even life-changing, *Grit* is a book about what goes through your head when you fall down, and how that—not talent or luck—makes all the difference.

Grit scale quiz

http://angeladuckworth.com/grit-scale/

10 questions

Here are a number of statements that may or may not apply to you. There are no right or wrong answers, so just answer honestly, considering how you compare to most people. At the end, you'll get a score that reflects how passionate and persevering you see yourself to be.

The good news about this brief Grit score is that you don't have to register or give them your email. Take the quiz – get your score. Cool.

13 Things Mentally Strong People Don't Do

by Amy Morin

Blinkist:

13 Things Mentally Strong People Don't Do (2014) describes how you can take control of your emotions, thoughts and actions and develop greater mental strength. With useful tips, inspiring examples and practical solutions, this book will help you overcome your fears and start living life to the fullest.

Publisher's Summary:

Everyone knows that regular exercise and weight training lead to physical strength. But how do we strengthen ourselves mentally for the truly tough times? And what should we do when we face these challenges? Or as psychotherapist Amy Morin asks, what should we avoid when we encounter adversity? Through her years counseling others and her own experiences navigating personal loss, Morin realized it is often the habits we cannot break that are holding us back from true success and happiness. Indulging in self-pity or agonizing over things beyond our control, obsessing over past events, resenting the achievements of others, or expecting immediate positive results all hold us back.

Now, for the first time, Morin expands upon the *13 Things* from her viral post, and shares her tried-and-true practices for increasing mental strength. Increasing your mental strength can change your entire attitude. It takes practice and hard work, but with Morin's specific tips, exercises, and troubleshooting advice, it is possible to not only fortify your mental muscle but also drastically improve the quality of your life.

©2015 Amy Morin (P)2015 HarperCollins Publishers

How to Stop Worrying and Start Living
by Dale Carnegie
Blinkist:

How to Stop Worrying and Start Living (1948) is a self-help classic that outlines clearly why worrying is bad for you and what you can do about it. With tools and techniques to put to action, as well as a wealth of examples and anecdotes to back up its recommendations, *How to Stop Worrying and Start Living* can help you worry less today.

Publisher's Summary:

Through Dale Carnegie's seven-million-copy best seller (recently revised) millions of people have been helped to overcome the worry habit. Dale Carnegie offers a set of practical formulas you can put to work today, formulas that will last a lifetime! Discover how to:

Eliminate 50 percent of business worries immediately

Reduce financial worries

Turn criticism to your advantage

Avoid fatigue and keep looking young

Add one hour a day to your waking life

Find yourself and be yourself - remember, there is no one on earth like you!

How to Stop Worrying and Start Living deals with fundamental emotions and ideas. It is fascinating to listen to and easy to apply. Let it change and improve you. There's no need to live with worry and anxiety that keep you from enjoying a full, active, and happy life!

How Will You Measure Your Life?

By Clayton M. Christensen, James Allworth and Karen Dillon

Blinkist:

As a leading business expert and cancer survivor, Clayton M. Christensen provides you with his unique insight on how to lead a life that brings both professional success and genuine happiness. In *How Will You Measure Your Life?* Christensen touches on diverse topics such as motivation and how you can harness it, what career strategy is the best for you, how to strengthen relationships with loved ones, and how to build a strong family culture.

Publisher's Summary:

In 2010, world-renowned innovation expert Clayton M. Christensen gave a powerful speech to the Harvard Business School's graduating class. Drawing upon his business research, he offered a series of guidelines for finding meaning and happiness in life.

He used examples from his own experiences to explain how high achievers can all too often fall into traps that lead to unhappiness.

The speech was memorable not only because it was deeply revealing but also because it came at a time of intense personal reflection: Christensen had just overcome the same type of cancer that had taken his father's life. As Christensen struggled with the disease, the question "How do you measure your life?" became more urgent and poignant, and he began to share his insights more widely with family, friends, and students.

In this groundbreaking book, Christensen puts forth a series of questions: How can I be sure that I'll find satisfaction in my career? How can I be sure that my personal relationships become enduring sources of happiness? How can I avoid compromising my integrity - and stay out of jail? Using lessons from some of the world's greatest businesses, he provides incredible insights into these challenging questions.

How Will You Measure Your Life? is full of inspiration and wisdom, and will help students, midcareer professionals, and parents alike forge their own paths to fulfillment.

©2012 Clayton M. Christensen, James Allworth, and Karen Dillon (P)2012 HarperCollinsPublishers

Finding Your Element
by Ken Robinson
Blinkist:
Finding Your Element (2013) offers engaging advice on ways you might discover your true passions and talents, and then reorient your life to incorporate more time for them. Written with a keen sense of wit, *Finding Your Element* offers entertaining and inspiring

wisdoms that will help you not only to be more productive but also to improve your overall happiness and quality of life.

Publisher's Summary:

Sir Ken Robinson's groundbreaking book The Element introduced listeners to a new concept of self-fulfillment through the convergence of natural talents and personal passions. The Element has inspired people all over the world and has created for Robinson an intensely devoted following. Now comes the long-awaited companion, the practical guide that helps people find their own Element. Among the questions that this new book answers are:

How do I find out what my talents and passions are?

What if I love something I'm not good at?

What if I'm good at something I don't love?

What if I can't make a living from my Element?

How do I do help my children find their Element?

Finding Your Element comes at a critical time, as concerns about the economy, education, and the environment continue to grow. The need to connect to our personal talents and passions has never been greater. As Robinson writes in his introduction, wherever you are, whatever you do, and no matter how old you are, if you're searching for your Element, this book is for you.

©2013 Ken Robinson and Lou Aronica (P)2013 Tantor

Emotional Intelligence

by Daniel Goleman

Blinkist:

Emotional Intelligence is a #1 bestseller with more than five million copies sold. It outlines the nature of emotional intelligence and shows its vast impact on many aspects of life. It depicts the ways emotional intelligence evolves and how it can be boosted. It poses an alternative to the overly cognition-centered approaches to the human mind that formerly prevailed in the psychological establishment. It presents the reader with new insights into the relationship between success and cognitive capabilities, and a positive outlook on possibilities to improve his life.

Publisher's Summary:

Everyone knows that high IQ is no guarantee of success, happiness, or virtue, but until Emotional Intelligence, we could only guess why. Daniel Goleman's brilliant report from the frontiers of psychology and neuroscience offers startling new insight into our "two minds" - the rational and the emotional - and how they together shape our destiny.

Through vivid examples, Goleman delineates the five crucial skills of emotional intelligence and shows how they determine our success in relationships, work, and even our physical well-being. What emerges is an entirely new way to talk about being smart.

The best news is that "emotional literacy" is not fixed early in life. Every parent, every teacher, every business leader, and everyone interested in a more civil society has a stake in this compelling vision of human possibility.

©2005 Daniel Goleman (P)2018 Daniel Goleman

The 21 Irrefutable Laws of Leadership

by John C. Maxwell

Blinkist:

The 21 Irrefutable Laws of Leadership (1998) explains what it takes to become a great leader. These blinks highlight many of the traits, skills and characteristics that have given leaders around the world the power to attract loyal followers and lead them toward success. Find out what Ray Kroc, Winston Churchill and Mother

Theresa all have in common – and what you can do to become a better leader yourself.

Publisher's Summary:

What would happen if a top expert with more than thirty years of leadership experience were willing to distill everything he had learned about leadership into a handful of life-changing principles just for you? It would change your life.

John C. Maxwell has done exactly that in *The 21 Irrefutable Laws of Leadership*. He has combined insights learned from his thirty-plus years of leadership successes and mistakes with observations from the worlds of business, politics, sports, religion, and military conflict. The result is a revealing study of leadership delivered as only a communicator like Maxwell can.

©2007 John C. Maxwell (P)2020 HarperCollins Leadership

All Marketers Are Liars

by Seth Godin

Blinkist:

All Marketers Are Liars explains how telling your customers authentic, meaningful stories about your business helps you sell your products and build a strong, long-lasting relationship with them.

Publisher's Summary:

Every marketer tells a story. And if they do it right, we believe them. We believe that wine tastes better in a $20 glass than a $1 glass. We believe that an $80,000 Porsche Cayenne is vastly superior to a $36,000 VW Touareg, which is virtually the same car. We believe that $225 Pumas will make our feet feel better, and look cooler, than $20 no-names... and believing it makes it true.

Successful marketers don't talk about features or even benefits. Instead, they tell a story. A story we want to believe.

This is a book about doing what consumers demand; painting vivid pictures that they choose to believe. Every organization, from nonprofits to car companies, from political campaigns to wineglass blowers, must understand that the rules have changed (again). In an economy where the richest have an infinite number of choices (and no time to make them), every organization is a marketer and all marketing is about telling stories.

Marketers succeed when they tell us a story that fits our worldview, a story that we intuitively embrace and then share with our friends. Think of the Dyson vacuum cleaner or the iPod.

But beware: If your stories are inauthentic, you cross the line from fib to fraud. Marketers fail when they are selfish and scurrilous, when they abuse the tools of their trade and make the world worse. That's a lesson learned the hard way by telemarketers and Marlboro.

This is a powerful book for anyone who wants to create things people truly want as opposed to commodities that people merely need.

©2005 Seth Godin (P)2005 Audible, Inc.

You Can Negotiate Anything
    by Herb Cohen
    Blinkist:
You Can Negotiate Anything (1980) shows that negotiations occur in every walk of life and that it is vital to have the skills and understanding to deal with those situations. The book outlines the key factors affecting negotiation success, as well as ways of negotiating for win-win solutions.

Amazon:

#1 New York Times bestseller: "If you are ever in a crucial life-changing negotiation, the person you want on your side of the table is Herb Cohen." (Time)

A nine-month New York Times bestseller with more than a million copies sold, *You Can Negotiate Anything* is the classic guide from Herb Cohen, who has been successfully negotiating everything from insurance claims to hostage releases, and hundreds of other matters, for over five decades. The man who coined the term "win-win," he has taught people the world over how to get what they want in any situation.

In clear, accessible steps, he reveals how anyone can use the three crucial variables of Power, Time, and Information to always reach a win-win outcome. No matter who you're dealing with, Cohen shows how every encounter is a negotiation that matters. With the tools and skill sets he has devised, honed, and perfected over countless negotiations, you can hone your intuition to effectively communicate and negotiate—and get the results you need.

Never Eat Alone
by Keith Ferrazzi
Blinkist:

In *Never Eat Alone*, Keith Ferrazzi, a successful businessman and marketing expert, takes us through the secrets to successful networking. He focuses on building lasting relationships rather than merely exchanging business cards, which seems to be many people's idea of networking today. He summarizes his findings in a system of tried and tested methods.

Publisher's Summary:

Do you want to get ahead in life? Climb the ladder to personal success? The secret, master networker Keith Ferrazzi claims, is in reaching out to other people. As Ferrazzi discovered in early life, what distinguishes highly successful people from everyone else is the way they use the power of relationships - so that everyone wins.

In *Never Eat Alone*, Ferrazzi lays out the specific steps – and inner mindset – he uses to reach out to connect with the thousands of colleagues, friends, and associates on his contacts list, people he has helped and who have helped him. And in the time since *Never Eat Alone* was published in 2005, the rise of social media and new, collaborative management styles have only made Ferrazzi's advice more essential for anyone hoping to get ahead in business.

©2014 John Ferrazzi (P)2014 Recorded Books

The 7 Habits of Highly Effective People

by Stephen R. Covey

Blinkist:

The Seven Habits of Highly Effective People (1989) is the enormously influential self-help phenomenon that can teach you the principles of effectiveness. Once you make these principles into habits, you'll be well on your way to more success, both in your personal and your professional life.

Change your habits and your life with this must-know self-help method beloved by millions.

Publisher's Summary:

Stephen R. Covey's book *The 7 Habits of Highly Effective People* has been a top seller for the simple reason that it ignores trends and pop psychology for proven principles of fairness, integrity, honesty, and human dignity. Celebrating its fifteenth year of helping people solve personal and professional problems, this special anniversary edition includes a new foreword and afterword written by Covey that explore whether the *7 Habits* are still relevant and answer some of the most common questions he has received over the past fifteen years.

©2004 Franklin Covey (P)2004 FranklinCovey

Chapter 22

Final Quote

"It is not the critic who counts; not the man who points how the strong man stumbles, or where the doer of deeds could have done them better. The credit belongs to the man who is actually in the arena, whose face is marred by dust and sweat and blood; who strives valiantly, who errs, who comes short again and again, because there is no effort without error and shortcoming; but who does actually strive to do the deeds; who knows great enthusiasm, the great devotions; who spends himself in a worthy cause; who at the best knows in the end the triumph of high achievement, and who at the worst, if he fails, at least fails while daring greatly, so that his place shall never be with those cold and timid souls who neither know victory or defeat."

Theodore Roosevelt
26th president of the United States (1858-1919)